Issues

in

Personality

Theory

Nevitt
Sanford

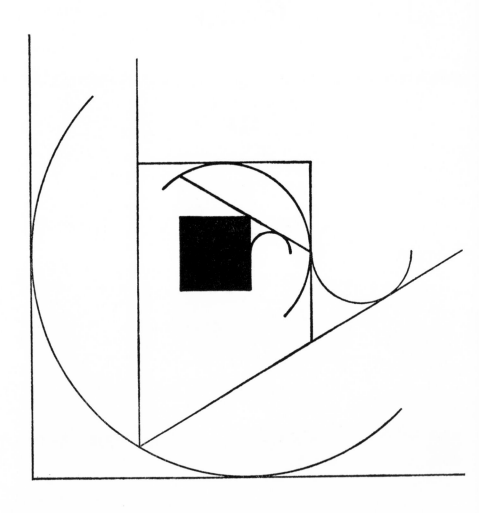

ISSUES
IN
PERSONALITY
THEORY

Jossey-Bass Inc., Publishers
615 Montgomery Street • San Francisco • 1970

THE JOSSEY-BASS BEHAVIORAL SCIENCE SERIES

General Editors

WILLIAM E. HENRY, *University of Chicago*

NEVITT SANFORD, *Wright Institute, Berkeley*

Preface

Recently I was reminded by an old friend that some psychologists question whether the field of personality still exists or at least whether it retains the promise of its early years. I had sent him a reprint, and when we met soon after that he commented, in a tone suggesting mischief more than surprise, "So, you're still doing personality." Of course my friend knows that personality is the subject of hundreds of lively courses, of hefty textbooks, and of innumerable current research papers. In suggesting that the study of personality is somehow outmoded, however, this man formulated a question which, if we merely shift its stress, may well be taken seriously by those of us who teach and do research in this field, namely, "Are we still doing *personality?*" Instead of abandoning the concept of personality, we ought to examine much more thoroughly its value and implications and to ask whether, in the kinds of research now done, we are meeting the challenge of that concept.

In *Issues in Personality Theory* I am guided not so much by a personal definition of personality as by a set of choices which we all face —choices about what we study, how we go about it, what forms of knowledge we seek, and for what purpose. I did not start with these issues as an outline but came upon them as I reviewed the bewildering variety of our field. In a sense, then, my topic is the kinds of choices we make as students of personality and some consequences of those choices. If our field has a structure, it consists less of common definitions or even purposes than of a cluster of implicit questions on which all of us take a stand, although we often choose by default.

In reviewing this book I wondered how our work as psychologists may affect the images which men have of themselves. I am referring not to our findings or to popularizations of them but rather to the model of man which we have developed to facilitate certain kinds of research. To what extent do our very methods of studying man imply views on the nature and possibilities of man? And to what extent do these views affect the self-images of our various publics? I suspect that the answer to each of these questions is *considerably*. We may well feel haunted by the irony of inadvertently changing the world less by our findings, highly specialized as they often are, than by the image of man implicit in our paradigm of science.

Whatever the dangers of an eventual science of behavior control, we ought to inquire now whether the images of man generated by our research needs may not deeply affect ideas about what man is and what he may become. As students of personality we ought to be developing a paradigm of research which respects the nature of man as a symbol-using, self-reflective creature who acts as well as behaves. We should ask ourselves whether the aim of our science is to control behavior, as some of us seem to assume, or to facilitate human development. To what extent are current models of "researchable man" a distortion of and a limitation upon human possibility?

These are some of the questions, by no means rhetorical, which I would ask readers to keep in mind while considering the choices which we face in doing research and which together form the structure of our field. In *Issues in Personality Theory* I isolate various choices, trace the direction of the main alternatives now recognized, and sketch some problems faced in each direction. The next step, and one I would urge on my readers, is to ask what image of man lurks in each alternative and what human values are thus embodied (or denied) in these images. These questions are awkward, recalcitrant, prickly; but how can we avoid them except by pretending that nobody believes the assumptions about man which we use to facilitate research or that, alone in the history of thought, we make no assumptions at all?

Issues in Personality Theory has been in preparation and under revision for more than ten years. It began to take shape in 1958, when Sigmund Koch asked me to write at length on the place of personality in psychology, a paper which eventually appeared in *Psychology: A Study of a Science* (Koch, 1963). At that time I made a fresh attempt to organize my lecture course in personality. Instead of orienting it around particular theories or around stages of development or in accord with a single theoretical system, I sought to base it on issues, which were ordered according to a broad, theoretically neutral conceptual scheme. Then, as now, I thought that as each area of personality theory grows more complicated and its literature more abundant, most of us prudently limit our area of special interest to keep up with the resulting flow of knowledge. This devotion to narrowly defined studies has brought some results which, if not always usable, are at least reliable within the frame of the experiment and are often theoretically tidy. No matter what our particular interests, however, we may gain perspective by shifting periodically from a close-up to a wide-angle lens and by seeking a new view of our field as a whole.

I have misgivings about attempting to present an overview of theory and research in the whole field of personality. This field, always complex, has expanded rapidly in the last decade and, in various forms, continues to do so. Often I merely broach here ideas that deserve to be treated at length. Instead of pausing over any of them, however, I move back to examine those aspects of the field which become visible only when we view the whole.

My image of this whole has not changed radically since I prepared the original paper. Indeed, reactions to that paper made me believe that I was on the right track and that continuing revision and elaboration were called for. In so doing, mainly in connection with my lecture course, I have retained the original scheme of elements, organization, boundaries, and relationships with other phenomena but have changed the order of topics and, I hope, have sharpened and clarified the issues. These issues have been remarkably persistent, though trends in thought and research may be noted. My experience has been that whereas the scheme has continued to be useful, my own changing interests and those of psychologists in general have led me to use at different times different details—different examples, different reports of research—for filling in the scheme. An instructor who wishes to make use of *Issues in Personality Theory* may do the same thing, that is, adopt the general plan offered here or some suitably modified version of it and then fill in with his substantive material. If he does, he may agree with me that the most recent work is not always to be preferred, that, indeed, contemporary research in personality often is so highly specialized and requires so much background in particular areas of inquiry that it is often less useful in a general course than are older investigations.

From my own experience, I also expect this instructor to find scope for the expression of his preferences with respect to theory. My general scheme is intended to be acceptable to psychologists of various theoretical persuasions; I have tried to leave behind my usual outlook, perhaps at the expense of skimping on my treatment of psychoanalytic concepts, which, when choice is necessary, I prefer; but no careful reader will fail to guess my views, for I do not hesitate to express opinions on or to judge the significance of ideas, methods, and findings. Still, in writing about trends or connections among events, I am not being arbitrary; for the most part, I am reporting facts of recent intellectual history, facts unmistakably significant for any estimate of progress in the field of personality.

Since this book has evolved in connection with courses at Berkeley and at Stanford, I owe a great deal to my students, who tolerantly held still while I tried out my ideas and then came forward with helpful criticisms. I owe most, however, to two men who helped me to organize and to teach my course. Paul Kanzer and Craig Comstock in succession and each for three years were my teaching assistants and intellectual companions at Stanford. Interested in pedagogy as well as in personality theory, they participated fully in my efforts at exposition as well as in my efforts to achieve conceptual clarity, and they influenced me almost as much as they think they did. Craig Comstock also read and criticized the manuscript more than once and helped to improve its prose. He has my best thanks.

I want also to thank Joseph Katz, John Kelton, and Peter Madison for their constant willingness to discuss personality theory, in ways that have been most helpful to me, and the following friends and colleagues who read the earliest version of the manuscript and made helpful suggestions: Donald Brown, Mervin Freedman, Walter Gruen, Richard Jung, Daniel Miller, Harvey Nash, Milton Rokeach, Brewster Smith, and Silvan Tomkins. For devoted specific help during the late stages of preparation warm thanks go to Patience Merian and Norbert Ralph. Support by the National Institute of Mental Health in the form of a Research Scientist Award (K5-MH-12, 829) is gratefully acknowledged.

Berkeley, California　　　　　　　　　　　　　　　NEVITT SANFORD
February 1970

Contents

Issues

in

Personality

Theory

ONE

Defining Personality

In company with most theorists in this field I assume that personality is an organized whole or system made up of elements or parts and separated somehow from an environment with which it interacts. Out of this simple working assumption arise fundamental questions which have occupied students of personality for a long time. These questions concern the nature of the elements of personality, or its theoretical variables; its principles of organization, which is to say the relationships among variables; the boundaries which mark personality off from other concepts such as behavior and the environment; and the relationships between personality and

1

other phenomena. In this book I mainly sketch the ways in which a variety of theorists have found it useful to deal with these questions. My purpose is not to offer a theory of my own or merely a quick summary of several theories, but rather to organize, as simply as I can, the major issues around which our thought and research seem to cluster.

This process of clustering is itself worthy of attention. During the past forty years, psychologists within our universities have developed a broad field of inquiry and teaching called personality. After discussing the theoretical issues of this broad field, I give some attention to its subdivisions and to its overlap with other fields of inquiry. In discussing overlaps, however, I confine myself to the relations between personality psychology and general psychology. If time and space were longer, it would be rewarding to consider the relations of personality to social psychology, to sociology and anthropology, and to abnormal or clinical psychology; but at least I am satisfied that in dealing with the relations of personality to general psychology, I have touched on issues that are no less fruitful than controversial.

In discussing such major areas as the elements of personality, their organization, and the transactions across boundaries, I first define central issues and consider proposals made by psychologists of various theoretical persuasions. This approach offers an opportunity to compare some of the most influential theories of personality, as well as a few which may deserve more attention than they have so far received. Then I note trends of thought and research in the area, going back over approximately four decades and looking ahead to the future. Just as I suggest the shape of the field as a whole, at the expense of slighting many aspects of it, I introduce the various issues through whatever examples seem most convenient, rather than trying, as I would in a full historical survey, to track down the origins or to footnote the most recent manifestations.

In discussing trends, I take the view that our choices respecting theory, problems, and method are influenced, sometimes covertly, by our ideas about the nature of science and in particular about the goals and prospects of psychology. The sociologists of knowledge and the historians of science may trace the origins and vicissitudes of these ideas, but here I try to confine my own curiosity and simply to sketch some ways in which our various images of psychology as a science and our career expectations (Adelson, 1969) may affect us as we decide on what research to do, what methods to use, and the kinds of theory we are developing.

First, though, we must deal with the question of what personality is. Like many words in common use, personality seems to have an obvious meaning or referent, but as Adams (1954) observes, all definitions of our subject use terms which themselves require definition. Adams gets the discussion started with an artful reference to one of the most common words in the language. "By the term *personality*," he writes, "I shall mean an entity of the sort you are referring to when you use the first person pronoun." Like the word *I*, personality is a concept with a lot of implications to be teased out of it, and perhaps we can begin to do so by considering a brief statement written by Schjelderup (1955) in his report of a follow-up study of people he had psychoanalyzed twenty to twenty-five years before.

Rather too briefly, but on the whole fitly, and in accordance with the results of this follow-up study, the personality changes effected by a successful analysis can be summed up in some such way as this: The more the neurotic inhibitions are dispelled and anxiety is extirpated, the more does natural self-consciousness emerge and the less stiff and cramped are the attitudes of the personality. The field of experience is enlarged, the attitude toward work and toward other people becomes more open and natural—without too much dependence, without exaggerated demands, but also without exaggerated modesty.

If the personality-changing aims of analysis were to be summed up in a simple formula, it might perhaps be Ibsen's: To be one's self. Or, to put it in other words: Analysis makes possible a higher degree of personality integration. [p. 118]

We are concerned not with whether Schjelderup defines all the terms he employs or offers sufficient evidence for the propositions stated, but rather with what he assumes his readers (psychologists, psychiatrists, social scientists) understand and take for granted respecting personality. The following thoughts are implicit in his statement.

Personality is a whole, embracing parts, or elements. (Attitudes, neurotic inhibitions, anxiety, and self-consciousness are of the personality.) We may make statements, as Schjelderup does, about personality in general, about *the* personality—any and all personalities. We may also remark on the state of the whole (its degree of integration, for example) and of particular parts (such as attitudes of the personality, which can be more or less stiff and cramped). The parts, or elements, of personality, apparently, are numerous and varied (neurotic inhibitions, anxiety, self-consciousness, attitudes, fields of experience, dependence, demands, modesty); and the same kind of part may be differentiated according to specific contents (an attitude toward work and an attitude toward other people, for example). Parts may vary in amount (neurotic inhibitions may be more or less dispelled, anxiety more or less extirpated); and like the whole, parts may vary in structure (attitudes may be stiff and cramped or open and natural, the field of experience may be large or small). Parts of the personality are related one to another formally (for example, parts may or may not be included in the field of experience, depending upon how large it is); and parts are also related dynamically in the sense that a change in one brings changes in others (as anxiety is extirpated, natural self-consciousness emerges, for example). Features of parts and of the whole and formal relationships among parts depend upon dynamic relationships among the parts. Because of neurotic inhibition and anxiety natural self-consciousness is submerged, attitudes are stiff and cramped, the field of experience is narrowed, and the personality as a whole is not integrated. Structural aspects of the whole and the parts are mutually related. For instance, in an integrated personality, attitudes are not stiff and cramped. Integration has to be defined, but we may assume for the moment that Schjelderup is using the term in its common meaning of bringing together of parts. We are saying that where there is maximum connectedness, the parts are characteristically open and natural rather than stiff and cramped.

In addition, personality is a more or less stable or enduring structure interacting with an environment. Were it not enduring we could not speak, as Schjelderup does, of the "changes effected by a successful analysis." Not mentioned by Schjelderup—but implied by his statement as a whole—is the existence of mechanisms by which neurotic inhibitions are dispelled and anxiety is extirpated and by which changes in attitude and in the field of experience are induced. Thus, it seems that personality, in whole and in part, interacts with an environment. Attitudes of personality are toward work and toward people; successful analysis and the use of verbal techniques in other forms of social interaction effect changes in personality—apparently by working directly upon neurotic inhibitions and anxiety. To list the kinds of changes that may occur is to sum up what has been said about the ways in which personality or its parts may vary in structure, in amount, and in dynamic relationships.

Finally, the functioning of personality as a whole and the functioning of its parts may be evaluated according to some criteria. Having a high degree of personality integration, apparently, is a healthy condition. The functioning of parts is good or bad according to whether it favors the integration of the whole. Too much dependence, exaggerated demands, and exaggerated modesty ought to be changed not so much because they are socially troublesome but because they are not open and natural; they are stiff and cramped and hence do not connect with other parts of the personality to make for its integration.

These assumptions seem to be fairly neutral with respect to current theory of personality, no doubt because Schjelderup's statement is so general as to be true of any system. But, even though Schjelderup is talking about the psy-

chological processes of persons, many current theorists probably
would not find much to disagree with here.

Some psychologists might object to the holistic orientation of the statement—not so much on principle as on the
ground that such an orientation is not conducive to research.
By holistic orientation I mean the disposition to view the personality as a whole and to consider that behavior can be fully
understood only in the context of this whole. (The organismic
point of view, to which reference is occasionally made here, is
essentially the same thing as holistic orientation.) Although
some presentations of a holistic point of view imply that the
whole personality or whole parts of it are not susceptible to
techniques of analysis, holism does not necessarily have this
implication. The essential idea is that living systems (cells, or-
gans, attitudes, the ego, personality) function as units. Any act
or performance of such systems involves systemwide processes;
therefore, the functioning of any part or subsystem depends
in some degree upon the functioning of the whole. The implication is not that wholes, such as the personality, cannot be
analyzed, but rather that analysis should include the exposition
of the relations of parts to the whole. The psychologist who
isolates a part function for intensive study should keep in mind
that he is abstracting from the whole.

The same kind of analysis that we have made of the
Schjelderup statement can be made of many contemporary statements about personality in which the authors have permitted
themselves to write at length and without defining their terms.
For example, in explaining the implications of their research
for the study of personality, Smith, Bruner, and White (1956)
made use of all the concepts and assumptions above. The
same assertion may be made about most contemporary case
studies.

Our concern is not to argue for an implicit agreement
among current views but to introduce terms that have a place
in discussions of how personality should be defined. We may
now examine some representative formal definitions approximately in the order in which they have appeared in the litera-

ture to see whether the terms already introduced are not the most important ones. It is conventional nowadays to begin with Allport's (1937b) definition:

Personality is the dynamic organization within the individual of those psychophysical systems that determine his unique adjustments to his environment. [*p. 48*]

However, previously Murphy and Jensen (1932) defined personality as the "whole dynamic system of tendencies which differentiate one person from another" (p. v).

Murray did not offer a single definition of personality in his early writings; rather, he considered personological phenomena in different contexts and proposed different definitions of personality at different times. But by bringing together several statements from *Explorations in Personality* (Murray, 1938), we may see what he meant by personology:

We were accustomed to conceive of personality as a temporal integrate of mutually dependent processes developing in time. . . . Personality is at all times an integral whole. . . . The constituent processes are functionally inseparable. [*pp. ix–x*] *. . . Since all complex adaptive behavior is evidently coordinated by excitations in the brain, the unity of the organism's development and behavior can be explained only by referring to organizations occurring in this region.* [*p. 45*] *. . . Personalities constitute the subject matter of psychology. . . . Personology, then, is the science of men, taken as gross units. . . . Since it (personology) has to do with the life histories of individuals (the largest unit) it must be most inclusive, other types of psychology being specialties or branches of it.* [*p. 4*] *. . . Because of the meaningful connection of sequences, the life cycle should be taken as a unit, the long unit for psychology. . . . The history of the organism is the organism.* [*p. 39*]

Another organismic, or holistic, conception of personality and one that is also field theoretical is that of Angyal (1941):

Personality [is] defined, dynamically, as the processes of living. [p. 374] . . . The life process does not take place within the body alone but includes the intrasomatic and extrasomatic happenings. . . . The realm in which the life process takes place has been called the "biosphere." . . . The biosphere is roughly differentiated into subject (organism) and object (environment). [p. 123] . . . We propose to study life as a unitary whole and endeavor to describe the organization and dynamics of the biosphere. [p. 100] . . . Personality can be regarded as a hierarchy of systems. In the larger personality organization the significant positions are occupied by constituents which themselves are also systems. [p. 186]

Lewin, another writer fully identified with holism and field theory, did not offer a formal definition of personality; rather, his conception emerges from his various writings. Bronfenbrenner (1951) offers a useful summary.

Lewin conceives of personality as a "differentiated region of the life space," a "more or less unitary and more or less closed" organization of interrelated psychical systems. Although he never formally defines the last concept, it is readily apparent from his discussion that the psychical system denotes a disposition to respond in a particular way to selective aspects of the psychical field. [p. 212]

Linton (1945), an anthropologist, is not explicitly holistic but his definition is certainly inclusive. Personality is taken to mean "the organized aggregate of psychological processes and states pertaining to the individual" (p. 84).

Krech and Crutchfield (1948) are mainly concerned to present a theory of the origins and development of personality, but they do not neglect, in their definition, the ideas of pattern and of uniqueness.

Characteristic modes of tension reduction are learned by the individual as a function of his past experiences of success or failure with them and of the opportunity for employment of them within the confines of his particular culture. Personality may be described as the pattern of relative importance of these various modes of adjustment to tension which uniquely characterizes the individual. [p. 73]

Newcomb (1950a) accents the interactions of personality and the social environment and focuses his attention upon the individual's behavior in social roles, but this viewpoint does not prevent his following Allport in making the concepts of disposition and of organization fundamental to his definition of personality.

Now personality, as I am sure we are all agreed, is known only as we observe individual behavior. (I am using the term "personality," by the way, in the inclusive sense of referring to the individual's organization of predispositions to behavior.) What I want to suggest is that the kind of behavior from which we can learn most about personality is role behavior. By observing John Doe in such capacities as husband, host, employee, and employer, we can discover those kinds of order and regularity in his behavior which are the goal of the student of personality. [p. 277]

Cattell (1950) makes the point that at this stage of our knowledge, only a denotative definition of personality is possible.

For this reason we may say: Personality is that which permits a prediction of what a person will do in a given situation. . . . Personality is . . . concerned with all the behavior of the individual, both overt and under the skin. [pp. 2–3]

McClelland (1951), more than other writers so far considered, seems to focus on behavior rather than on particular conceptions of what lies behind it. Personality is "the most adequate conceptualization of a person's behavior in all its detail that a scientist can give at a moment in time" (p. 69).

Eysenck's (1953) definition follows rather closely that of Allport.

Personality is the more or less stable and enduring organization of a person's character, temperament, intellect, and physique, which determines his unique adjustment to his environment. [p. 2]

And in Hilgard (1953) we find the same influence, but he is less like Allport and more like McClelland in accenting behavior rather than dispositions. For Hilgard, personality is

the sum total of individual characteristics and ways of behaving which in their organization or patterning describe an individual's unique adjustment to his environment. [p. 407]

Von Bertalanffy (1951), the general systems theorist, offers "a tentative definition of the living organism":

A living organism is a hierarchy of open systems maintaining itself in a steady state due to its inherent system conditions. . . . It appears that a corresponding definition could be applied as a general model of personality. [p. 37]

Sullivan (1953), who approaches the subject from the point of view of a psychiatrist, is like Newcomb in stressing the social nature of personality. He directs our attention to "the relatively enduring pattern of recurrent interpersonal situations which characterize a human life" (p. 111).

Finally, we may consider a contemporary definition based on an attempted integration of the most important theories of personality. Bronfenbrenner (1951) offers:

A conception of personality as a system of relatively enduring dispositions to experience, discriminate, or manipulate actual or perceived aspects of the individual's environment (including himself). [p. 158]

Psychoanalytic writers from Freud (1938) on have conceived of personality as synonymous with the psyche, and their theories of personality have been general psychological theories. Thus for Freud (1927, 1930, 1936) in his later, functionalist phase, the personality is made up of the three major systems—the id, the ego, and the superego—the interactions of which determine behavior. For Jung (1954) also, the personality is made up of interacting systems, the principal ones being the ego, the personal unconscious, and the shadow. For Fairbairn (1952), a British psychoanalyst in the tradition of Klein, personality is a system comprising the ego and internalized objects.

Without unfairly or incorrectly committing any of the above writers to holistic views it is possible to say that for all of them personality is something, usually a very inclusive or comprehensive something, embracing parts, elements, processes, subsystems, or characteristics, which are organized or patterned. (What the elements are, how they are to be conceptualized, and how they are organized is another story.)

Within this broad area of agreement, we can find, of course, many differences. With reference to the time perspective, some writers accent the organization of processes at a given moment, others the organization or patterning of sequences of events over long periods. These differences, however, do not seem to be a matter for any theoretical controversy; writers who study the organization of life cycles are not inclined to slight organization as of any given moment, and writers who focus upon the personality of the moment are not inclined to deny its lawful relations to the past and future. There is also lack of agreement respecting the uniqueness of each personality and of its adjustments to its environment. Some writers consider it important to mention this aspect (or supposed aspect) of personality, and others do not. This, as we shall see, is a controversial matter. We may also note differences in the way writers delimit personality. Even the brief definitions given above suggest a variety of different conceptions of the boundaries of personality. Does it or does it not include overt behavior, the products of behavior, some parts or features of an environment, physique and physiological functioning, character, temperament, intelligence?

These, then, are the topics discussed here: the kinds of elements, the manner of their organization, and the problem of boundaries, as well as the questions of uniqueness and of change over time.

TWO

Elements
of Personality

Proposals of units in which personality might be analyzed have been many and varied during the history of psychology. Many proposals are still in good standing. Our task here is to discuss the nature of the problem of analysis, to offer a brief survey of the proposals, to point out some considerations other than purely theoretical ones that have shaped the conceptualization of elements, and to note, if possible, any trends in theory and in research.

Angyal (1941) points out four possible ways to divide a whole object for study. One can make random cuts and obtain a number of fragments; one can divide the whole accord-

13

ing to a previously fixed principle which does not take into account the intrinsic nature of the whole (dividing a tree into inch cubes); one can "divide" by abstraction, resolving the object into a number of distinguishable properties or features such as color, weight, or consistency; finally one can divide the whole according to the structure of the whole itself, for example, a building may be divided into corridors, rooms, windows, and doors. Psychologists have attempted all these ways of dividing personality.

The practice of making cuts in accord with an interest of the moment is a common one that has obvious advantages. For example, certain dispositions in the person (but not, in this case, abstracted features of the whole person) may be chosen for investigation or assessment because of their practical importance. As in the case of the wartime Office of Strategic Services assessment work (OSS Assessment Staff, 1948), psychologists of quite different theoretical orientations can cooperate in the assessment of such dispositions and in investigations of their value as predictors of future performances because no one is required to commit himself to a theory concerning either the definition or the determinants of such dispositions or of their relations in the personality. The same can be said for the development, by strictly empirical means, of tests to predict socially relevant kinds of behavior—an enterprise that is still flourishing, as in the Minnesota Multiphasic Personality Inventory (Baron, 1953a, 1953b, 1953c; Gough, 1957; Hathaway and McKinley, 1943; Webster and Heist, 1959; Center for the Study of Higher Education, 1962).

Such proceedings are theoretically quite neutral; all that need be assumed is that personality has certain regularities of functioning that are expressed in consistent behavior and that make prediction possible. Facts obtained in this empirical way, apart from their possible practical usefulness, may later find a useful place in a theoretical formulation of personality if the means by which they were obtained were indeed strictly empirical.

The practice of dividing personality according to a

fixed principle that ignores the nature of the whole is rarely, if ever, encountered in pure form in contemporary psychology of personality. The older stimulus-response psychology, according to which personality was simply the total of the basic stimulus-response connections, and the older faculty approach to personality were rather good examples of this mode of dividing an object. Modern stimulus-response theory (Dollard and Miller, 1950; Miller, 1959; Mowrer, 1950; Osgood, 1956, 1957; Sears, 1951a, 1951b; Shaffer and Shohen, 1956) shows much awareness of the complexity of personality and has been concerned to introduce concepts which explain how stimulus-response elements are built up into larger wholes. Similarly, modern factor analysis (Cattell, 1950; Eysenck, 1947; Guilford, 1959) proceeds in accordance with a conceptual model of personality functioning.

Abstracted features of the whole personality (soundness, stability, maturity, harmoniousness) are often used as variables. Indeed, they creep almost inevitably into the discussion as soon as one devotes particular attention to any one individual. The use of such variables usually involves no commitment to any theoretical position; psychologists can agree to use the variables while differing in their formulations of the states, processes, and relationships that give rise to them. Usually such variables are measured poorly, if at all. To appraise such features of a personality as soundness or stability obviously requires a rather thoroughgoing understanding of that personality, one that can be attained only by intensive study over time. Psychologists have not studied personalities in this way very often, but—unable to proceed without reference to abstracted features of the whole—they have made do with ratings of them.

Psychologists have rarely undertaken to derive elements strictly in accordance with the principle of structural articulation. Instead of starting with a conception of the whole personality and then seeking to divide it along lines suggested by a theory of its organization, they have commonly started with a general theory of behavior and then simply transposed to

personality whatever units of analysis have been adopted—
habits for stimulus-response theories (Dollard and Miller, 1950;
Mowrer, 1950), needs for functionalist theories (Murray, 1938;
Maslow, 1954), regions for gestalt theories (Cartwright, 1959;
Lewin, 1935). Sears (1950) considers this sound practice, while
Allport (1943) calls it wholly unsuitable.

One may ask whether this practice is not an example
of division according to an irrelevant fixed principle. I think
this is not often clearly the case; as suggested above, most contemporary personality theorists who employ units of this kind
are concerned about the functional roles of these units in the
organization of personality. Whether there is division according to an irrelevant fixed principle would have to be shown
on the basis of careful analysis of particular cases.

The fact remains, however, that starting with the whole
is not the American way. A serious attempt to derive elements
by taking the intrinsic nature of the whole into account would
differ sharply from the prevailing emphasis on the measura-
bility of personality variables and on the predictability of behavior in concrete situations. For the best examples of division
by structural articulation, we have to go back to the psychoanalytic theories of Freud (1927) and of Jung (1954). Each of
these psychologists divided the psyche into several major systems and propounded theory according to which the nature of
the whole was expressed in the interactions among these systems. Thus, none of Freud's three major systems—id, superego,
ego—can be defined without reference to the others and to the
whole personality. Jung's major subsystems—persona, personal
unconscious, collective unconscious, ego, self—have not caught
on with psychologists interested in empirical work—a fact that
Jung did not find disappointing. (His abstracted features of
introversion and extroversion have, of course, often been
studied empirically.) Freud's subsystems, on the other hand,
were defined with considerable reference to behavior, and the
research psychologist has found that they could stimulate empirical work. No one claims to have measured characteristics
of the superego with precision, but doing so is not different

from finding behavioral indexes of other hypothetical constructs, such as needs. These crude notions have persisted largely because psychologists do have occasion, particularly in clinical practice, to conceive of whole personalities, and for this purpose, better concepts than Freud's have not as yet come along.

The practice of deriving elements of personality from general theories of behavior in the belief that there is just one psychology has been severely criticized by theorists such as Allport (1937a; 1937b) who argue for a distinctive personality psychology and for units of analysis derived from a consideration of the nature of personality itself. In the thirties it was not difficult to distinguish between general psychology and the psychology of personality. At that time general psychology was concerned mainly with the generalized adult mind and focused largely upon laboratory studies of learning and perception. It left molar behavior, motivation, and a wide range of processes brought over from the clinic to the personality psychologist. Today the most typical phenomena of personality—motivation and the relations of motives to other phenomena such as forgetting—are just as general and are just as worthy of attention from general psychologists as are the more familiar phenomena of learning and perception. Behavior theorists hold that personality psychology and the general psychology of behavior are coextensive. They have been joined by gestalt psychologists and in particular those who espouse the topological psychology of Lewin (1935), whose *Dynamic Theory of Personality* was wholly taken up with the effort to establish general laws governing processes in a field that contained variables both in the person and in the psychological environment.

Some writers, admitting the force of the argument for generality but wishing to save something for a psychology of personality, take the view that the field of personality owes its distinctiveness solely to its concern with individual differences and the unique organization of each individual. Others—the great majority of those fully identified with the study of personality—claim that an adequate general psychology can be nothing other than a psychology of personality. The latter is a traditional view of the matter. Certainly Freud and Jung considered that personality was synonymous with mind or psyche and that their theories were general psychological ones. Murray (1938), Goldstein (1939), and Angyal (1941) took the same position when, in the 1930s, they espoused the organismic point of view. Following these older statements, contemporary writers such as Maslow (1954), Rogers (1959), Cattell (1950), and von Bertalanffy (1951) assume (1) that since all behavior depends on varying processes in the person as well as on the situation, there can be no general psychological laws that do not take relatively enduring personality processes into account, and (2) that no particular process, such as establishing a conditional reflex or perceiving another individual, can be fully understood apart from the context of the total system of the person.

Allport (1937b) noted that of all the practices described above the most significant and important proposals proceed from some general theory of the mental life. For example, some of the proposals were based on stimulus-response elements, and others on uniform (nomothetic) elements, including faculties, elements of general psychology (habits, images, feelings), and dynamic elements of the nomothetic order such as Murray's "needs." Allport was critical of both these elements: of those in the latter group because they are not distinctly personal or unique to the individual; and of those in the first group because they make insufficient allowance for the generality and complexity of personal dispositions. As his idea of a suitable element for the analysis of personality, he introduced the concept of trait, a biophysical, generalized, functionally autonomous, concrete, and personal determining tendency.

Since 1937, when Allport made his interpretation, the search for elements of personality has continued apace, and although the dilemmas confronting the theorist seem to be about the same now as then, we can detect some trends in thought and in research. For one thing, theorists seem to be considerably more aware of each other today than they were earlier. Allport could point to various schemes for the analysis of the total personality and note that they scarcely overlapped. Today there is much more overlapping. The contemporary writer—even though he may be primarily an exponent of one of the classical theories of personality, such as the stimulus-response, psychoanalytic, and field theoretical ones—is very likely to try to show that his scheme may be reconciled with other schemes or that it takes into account or thoroughly embraces their important features. To be sure, a certain amount of theoretical imperialism persists, and a writer may implicitly invite others to share his assumption that his scheme is a better formulation of what the others are getting at, but even here there seems to be very considerable awareness of other approaches.

An aspect of this increase in mutual awareness among theorists is the tendency of each to strive for comprehensiveness—to include in his scheme the products of other people's thought and research. Murray (1959), for example, acknowledged his indebtedness to colleagues in sociology and anthropology for helping him bring his theory into line with current thinking about man in society. Again, Cattell (1959) is best known as a trait psychologist or factor theorist, but he seems to have no difficulty including conceptions from dynamic psychology and psychoanalysis in his scheme.

Preferences and practices in choosing units for the analysis of personality depend not only upon the investigator's orientation to theory but also on the interests of the investigator, the kinds of problems he sets himself, and the kinds of observations he makes. When, for example, the psychologist addresses himself to practical problems involving people, he is likely to use less abstract categories than those that appeal to the experimentalist or to the devotee of elegant theory. Thus the psychotherapist when faced with the necessity for taking action affecting a person, often on short notice, has to deal with the relatively concrete and particular without stopping to translate his thoughts into the terms of a general theoretical system. Again, some students of personality are interested primarily in persistent differences among people, others in changes in the same people over time. The former prefer to investigate variables such as abilities or temperamental traits that are presumably either genetically or somatically linked or else highly generalized and pervasive; the latter prefer elements such as social attitudes, values, and opinions that, according to theory, are correlated with experience.

In sum, all agree that elements must be conceived and their attributes or characteristics measured; but disagreement about the nature of these elements has been marked throughout the history of personality psychology, and it shows no signs of ending soon. The disagreement exists mainly because elements, being invisible, are naturally conceptualized differently by many different personality theorists and because the measurement of elements is methodologically very difficult; poorly conceived elements cannot be exposed for what they are, and psychologists are too often guided by what existing methods can measure rather than by what is essential to theory. Disagreement has stimulated much theoretical work and empirical research directed to the discovery and the examination of elements of personality. Progress will be made as behavior theorists become interested in studying complex structures and as dynamic-organismic theorists improve their methodological sophistication.

Consistent with this increase in theoretical and empirical work is an increased sense of the complexity of personality, combined with a widespread perception of the relative newness of this field and an increased sense of modesty about what we can hope to accomplish in the immediate future. Great minds have labored and left us not a general scheme that all can tentatively accept but a variety of competing schemes which all seem to have some merit. Every day there is a fresh call for a general theory of personality, but not many psychologists seem willing to take on the task of creating one. There is much disagreement concerning the kind of theory or, more particularly, the kind of conceptual model that we ought to have (Brand, 1954; Eysenck, 1952; Feigl and Scriven, 1956; Klein and Krech, 1951; McCary, 1956; MacKinnon, 1953; MacKinnon and Maslow, 1951; Parsons and Shils, 1952; Rapaport, 1959; Spence, 1944; Tolman, 1951; von Bertalanffy, 1951). This discussion increases our sophistication about theory-making, but perhaps at the same time our cautiousness about offering anything more than a preliminary or tentative outline or sketch also increases. It is not that eclecticism is particularly valued; on the contrary, "having a theory" or "starting with a theory" seems very much the favored thing. It is rather that psychologists seem somewhat humbled before and frustrated by the vastness of the problem.

Happily, this state of affairs does not seem to have put any brakes upon research in the field. We can operationally define innumerable variables of personality in terms of consistency in behavoir, hypothesize some underlying regularity of functioning, and state some theory with which one can predict certain relationships with fair accuracy. One cannot study everything at once in any case, and one hopes that facts discovered in this way may someday find a place within an over-all formulation.

Dynamic elements of the nomothetic order have continued to be the most typical variables of personality. Personality theorists traditionally have preferred a functionalist point of view, or action frame of reference (Parsons, Bales, and Shils, 1953; Parsons and Shils, 1952), a way of looking at behavior that gives a central place to strivings that are important to the survival, growth, and identity of the organism (Bruner, 1951; Frenkel-Brunswik, 1951; Klein, 1956; McDougall, 1908, 1932; Miller, 1951; Murray, 1938; Rapaport, 1959). To survive, grow, and have an identity in the complex and changing environment that is every person's lot involves the setting and achieving of diverse goals. The individual learns goals and techniques that are successful in reducing tension, removing stress, or maintaining equilibrium, and they become characteristic modes of striving for him. Thus all theories of personality posit a multiplicity of motives as more or less durable attributes of the person. Psychologists differ about the fundamental nature of striving, the number of different motives that should be conceptualized, the manner in which they are learned, the degree of their generality, and the nature of their relations—but few doubt that motives exist as elements of personality.

The functional point of view has many immediate implications. The conception of an organism striving in a complex environment and learning in accordance with experiences of success and failure is the basis for the formulation of many variables of personality. Functionalists commonly distinguish goal states (conditions of reduced tension or equilibrium with concomitant gratification) from goal objects (objects—to use the broadest sense of the term—that become important because of their role in attaining goal states) and distinguish both goal states and goal objects from instrumentalities, techniques, or devices calculated to further the attainment of goals. This differentiation becomes the basis for three broad classes of personality variables: motives (needs, impulses, drive states), motive-object combinations (sentiments, object relations, attitudes, values—in certain common senses of these words), and instrumental traits (modes, styles).

This breakdown does not meet with universal approval. Opinions differ as to which of the above terms are to be preferred and how they are to be defined. And more than this, clearly the same phenomena may be dealt with on different levels of analysis; for example, habits may be identified in each of the three areas. But this explanation will have to suffice as a rough statement about some of the major elements of personality that proceed from the prevailing functionalist point of view.

In recent years the accent upon motives has decreased and the accent upon cognitive variables of personality has increased. According to the functionalist point of view, the cognitive processes of a person are in the service of his adaptive needs. A long tradition of personality research has attempted to show the influence of motivational factors, such as needs, sentiments, attitudes, and values, upon various cognitive functions, ranging from the perception of differences among weights to the building of systems of belief (Adorno and others, 1950; Bruner and Goodman, 1947; Frenkel-Brunswik, 1949; Klein and Schlesinger, 1949; Murray, 1933; Postman, Bruner, and McGinnies, 1948; Proshansky and Murphy, 1937a, 1956; Smith, Bruner, and White, 1956; Witkin and others, 1953). The numerous cognitive variables of personality that have been posited —ideologies, belief systems, cognitive structures—have been seen as having a functional role in the over-all adjustment of the individual.

This frame of reference in psychology, though it has long had its exponents within academic psychology (for example, McDougall, 1908, 1932), has been most characteristically the psychology of the clinic; its rise to influence in the general field of psychology is a part of the history of clinical psychology. In the thirties and forties, the efforts of the functionalists to put across their point of view were a source of considerable excitement within the ranks of academic psychologists. Today the functionalists' struggle seems largely to have been won; they are able to relax, even to inquire whether cognitive functions do not deserve attention as variables in their own right, as variables having perhaps a certain independence of motives. In these circumstances, the long-time experts in cognition (Asch, 1952; Bruner, 1957; Heider, 1958; Luchins, 1951; Sheerer, 1954; Wallach, 1949) have, of course, come in for their innings.

Today cognition is being studied both as a motive in its own right and as a function independent of motive, having its own laws and developmental history and possibly interacting with motive. The need to know, to find meaning, to achieve some structure in the world one perceives was first brought to prominence by Bartlett (1932), was reemphasized by Tolman (1948), and has recently been used by Kelly (1953) as the fundamental postulate in a whole system of psychology. In Kelly's system, the cognitive process of anticipating events—far from being merely in the service of more fundamental needs—is itself a disposition so fundamental that many of the so-called basic psychological needs may operate in its service. Aggression, for example, may be understood as an effort to force events to go according to one's expectations.

To put so much emphasis on the striving aspect of cognition is different from merely observing that cognition is part of human nature or from saying, with Krech and Crutchfield (1948), that "man is an organizing animal as far as his perceptions are concerned." With less emphasis on striving, cognition is seen not as determining molar behavior but as entering into the determination of all behavior and as setting the limits within which motivations may operate. If what a man knows depends on what he needs, so may his needs depend on what he knows or believes or expects. If man cannot help but cognize, and if, through cognizing, he builds up a fund of experience, then what he knows, believes, and expects at any given time depends heavily upon what his environment has chanced to put in his way. Thus an accent on cognition usually goes with an accent on the environment rather than on personality needs as a determinant of behavior. And if a man sets his goals in accordance with his experience, then clearly many of his motives depend upon his past or present cognitive functioning. Consequently, an accent on cognition tends to accompany an accent on conscious—as opposed to unconscious—processes and, with respect to the life history of the individual, an accent on later rather than on earlier events in explaining the development of personality.

Interestingly, there is also a new willingness to give cognitive processes their due—perhaps more than their due—in psychoanalysis, perhaps the most functionalist, or action-oriented, of all functionalist psychologies. This emphasis is seen in the contemporary preoccupation of American writers with what the psychoanalysts call ego psychology (Gill, 1959; Hartmann, Kris, and Loewenstein, 1947; Rapaport, 1958). This new psychology, set forth by Hartmann, Kris, and Loewenstein (1947), argues that the ego, which embraces diverse cognitive functions, does not emerge from the id but has its own independent origins and course of development.

This is not the place to go into the theoretical issues involved. The main point here is that virtually all personality theorists today are at considerable pains to conceptualize cognitive variables of personality, such as beliefs, opinions, expectations, conceptions, ideologies, or cognitive habits, structures, systems, and "maps." Owing to the new inclination to assign these cognitive variables varying amounts of autonomy or even the status of determinants of goals, theorists have a fresh appreciation of the complexity of the relationships within the personality.

The accent on cognitive variables, though it has its independent history, may be viewed as part of a larger current emphasis on the higher mental processes and upon the distinctively human (as opposed to the animal) in man. In large part, this trend is a reaction against behaviorism and psychoanalysis. If these two schools of thought have emphasized such "low" things as instincts and impulses and automatic conditioning, the new trend accents man's "higher" nature, his rationality, his self-consciousness. This trend shows the influence of gestalt psychology, which states that the higher processes are usually larger wholes considered to have as much "reality" as the elementary processes to which psychoanalysis and behaviorism would "reduce" all phenomena. This trend of thought has been supported by certain trends in research and practice, even as it has helped to stimulate them. Of great importance has been the intensive study of normal—and superior—people, with the use of methods and concepts derived primarily from the clinic (Barron, 1954; Holt and others, 1958; Kelly and Fiske, 1951; Macfarlane, Allen, and Honzik, 1954; Maslow, 1950; Murray, 1938; Sanford, 1956b, 1966; Stern, Stein, and Bloom, 1956; Terman and Oden, 1947, 1959). This kind of research began with Murray's (1938) early work at the Harvard Psychological Clinic, pure research into the functioning of the normal personality as a whole. Personality assessment since then, beginning with the OSS venture (OSS Assessment Staff, 1948), has usually had the practical goal of selecting individuals for social roles in which they will be "effective," a goal which puts the accent on "positive" competencies, virtues, resources, and the like.

Paralleling this development has been the spread of the notion, in America, that psychotherapy is a means not merely for treating ailments or relieving suffering but for providing a positive good to more than a favored few. The rise of clinical psychology and its interest in defining a distinctive role for itself has combined with (and been nurtured by) the traditional American interest in self-improvement. The result has been a climate in which the aims of psychotherapy and the goals of personality development are matters of lively concern (Balint, 1948; Barron, 1954; Erikson, 1955; Jahoda, 1950, 1958; Maslow, 1950; Murphy, 1958; Sanford, 1955; Scott, 1958; Senn, 1950; Smith, 1959; Szasz, 1959, 1960; White, 1952; Whitehorn, 1959). A means for defining these aims and goals has been found in the idea of growth (Erikson, 1950, 1955, 1959; White, 1952). Sometimes growth toward such objectives as autonomy, stable self-identity, and integration is regarded as "natural" (White, 1952; Erikson, 1959); sometimes it is regarded merely as change, under the impact of culture, in directions valued in this particular society (Sanford, 1966). In either case, the psychotherapist has found himself allied with developmental psychologists and specialists in child training and education, whose chief concern is with the conditions favoring or hampering certain developmental desiderata.

Psychoanalysts and behaviorists of the twenties and thirties would probably have been horrified to be told that they were reducing the image of man and showing a woeful disregard for his potential. They would have been justified in thinking that by attending to neglected aspects of man's nature and by contributing facts and theories that explained his behavior, they were at long last offering that noble creature some means for controlling himself. Psychologists identified with these schools of thought today may well deny that their schemes are essentially nonhumanistic or inadequate to deal with man's higher functions, or they may argue that the whole issue of higher versus lower is, in the context of science, meaningless. But the fact remains that their critics (for example, G. W. Allport, 1955; Asch, 1952; Kelly, 1953; Maslow, 1954; Rogers, 1959) have gone on to conceptualize variables of personality that are designed to deal with the social, the mature, and the rational aspects of man—all of which had small place in the older scheme.

These differences in general outlook are reflected in theory and thus in conceptualizations affecting all the variables of personality. Thus if we are to follow Maslow (1955), we have to posit not only the usual drive-reduction (deficit) motives but growth motives as well; if we are to follow the modern trend in cognitive psychology, we must put the accent not so much on illusions, projections, and other need-driven distortions of reality as on processes of perception and on the mature, rational, and complicated cognitive structures; and if we are to follow one of the main dynamic theories of personality, we must put relatively less emphasis upon the defensive activities of the ego and relatively more emphasis upon its constructive, positively adaptive functions.

Where the accent is on the positive, the healthy, the mature, the socially valuable, and so on, it is necessary to speak of features of the whole personality. In order to appraise efficiency, creativity, autonomy, and the like, we must observe the whole person engaged in transactions with his environment; and by regarding the whole person as a system, we are able to gain some appreciation of his differentiation, integration, flexibility, resilience, soundness, and breadth.

Psychologists who accent higher mental processes give a large place to the concept of self. In the recent literature of research and theory, this concept has attained very considerable prominence (Allport, 1943; Bertocci, 1945; Chein, 1944; Hilgard, 1949; Rogers, 1951, 1959; Sarbin, 1952; Sherif and Cantril, 1947; Smith, 1950; Combs and Snygg, 1959; Stephenson, 1953; Symonds, 1951; White, 1948). In much of this literature self and ego are discussed together. Some writers regard the two terms as synonymous; others use them to refer to different phenomena, although one writer's self may closely resemble another's ego. Writers who employ both self and ego as different concepts usually consider the two to be related—with different degrees of intimacy. Some writers get by with only one of these concepts; in this case, the one embraces much the same phenomena that other writers treat with the use of both concepts.

Perhaps the present state of affairs is not quite so hopelessly confused as this. Two quite different trends in personality theory seem to have converged, and the process of sorting out the contributions of the two has not yet been completed. Psychologists of the functionalist persuasion, conceiving of the personality as embodying a multiplicity of strivings, have always recognized the likelihood of conflict among the strivings and between the strivings and the environment. Hence, they have found it necessary to conceive of mechanisms or processes through which the activities of the person were regulated. The regulating functions—inhibition, scheduling, reality-testing, decision-making, and the like—have usually been thought to constitute a system, such as the ego in psychoanalysis and in modern dynamic theory of personality.

At the same time, awareness of oneself has long been regarded as a particularly salient aspect of human experience. As Adams (1954) points out, an individual can get a good preliminary idea of what is meant by personality itself by examining what he means when he uses the pronoun *I*. But Adams would not argue that this content of awareness is all there is to personality or even that all the regulatory processes often called ego necessarily find their way into awareness. Thus most contemporary writers clearly distinguish a group of processes usually called ego functions from a content of awareness that the perceiving individual refers to as his self.

Each of these conceptions supplies the basis for numerous variables of personality. To the long list of psychoanalytic mechanisms, as we have seen, academic psychologists have been wont to add various more constructive, more integrative, or fundamentally more adaptive functions. Various so-called ego functions have been distinguished (Freud, 1937; Murray and Kluckhohn, 1955; Rapaport, 1959; Sanford, 1955; Symonds, 1946), and these are considered to vary in prominence and effectiveness from one individual to another. The ego is regarded as a system in some sense of this term (perhaps usually as a set of related variables), allowing an ascription to the ego of all the properties and the attributes that could be ascribed to any system.

With respect to the experience of self, it has been possible to distinguish numerous variables of content and organization—what features are ascribed, how they are patterned, how this pattern is valued, how consistent it is over time, and so on. The self has also been conceived as a system embracing subsystems, and hence in terms of variables such as differentiation, integration, breadth, and rigidity. If the self of awareness (the perceived or conceived self, the phenomenal self, or the self image) is strictly a matter of individual experience, then it seems proper enough to ask—as many psychologists have— what processes underlie this experience or other experiences. And it seems proper to make inferences concerning these processes. Hilgard (1949), for example, uses the concept of the inferred self, a complex structure or structures. If a psychologist should succeed in mapping this "real" self by appropriate techniques, he would be in a position to appraise the discrepancies between what is really there and what the subject experiences.

In the common view, there is considerable affinity between the self of awareness and the processes usually ascribed to the ego. In the classical psychoanalytic view, the ego is the part of the personality that is closest to consciousness and in closest touch with the external world. Some of its major functions, such as intending and decision-making, help give the individual the impression that his self is determining what he will do; and he is likely to exclude from his self-conception any processes (such as primitive impulses or readinesses to respond automatically to threats of punishment) which in the psychoanalytic view do not belong to the ego. This conception certainly argues for considerable overlap between conscious ego processes and the self of awareness. On the other hand, no writer who systematically regards the ego as a set of regulative processes considers that all these processes are represented in awareness. Nor is it usually held that the processes underlying the phenomenal self are limited to the ego processes.

Thus four major conceptions that have some currency and respectability emerge: ¹the self of awareness, or the phenomenal self; ²the set of all regulative processes and mechanisms, often considered to be related and to constitute an ego system; ³the regulative processes and mechanisms that enter into awareness and become candidates for inclusion in the phenomenal self; ⁴and the inferred self, the aggregate of processes underlying the phenomenal self. Obviously, none of the first three of these conceptions is coterminous with personality itself, and none is so considered. Rather, they are parts, or elements, of the whole—but they are complex parts and may be "divided" by analysis according to some theory of their structure and functioning or by abstraction of some of their features. The inferred self would appear to come close to being the same as personality. The individual may conceivably incorporate anything about the personality into his phenomenal self. On the other hand, he may make similar use of some things that are not in his personality—his body or certain features of his environment, perhaps what others mistakenly attribute to him or what he mistakenly appropriates, for example.

This brief account, focused as it is upon candidates for the status of an element of personality, rather bypasses the lively theoretical controversy that marks the whole area of the self and the ego. Much of the controversy concerns the origins and determinants of the self and the ego and their relations to the rest of the personality; hence it is not particularly relevant to a survey of elements. One of the main differences of opinion concerns how many of the functions that psychoanalysts and psychoanalytically oriented psychologists attribute to the ego may more properly be attributed to the phenomenal self. In general, of course, writers who emphasize what we have called the higher things are inclined to attach more importance to the phenomenal self. Here, as much as in any area of personality psychology, controversy and confusion flourish in the absence of suitable objective indexes of the hypothetical constructs with which we are concerned. If there were sufficient methodological access to the ego and to the inferred self, theoretical issues could be turned quickly into empirical questions.

Contemporary writing about the self and about the ego is holistic. For a long time psychologists have doubted their ability to analyze any thing so global as the whole personality and thus have tended to scoff at attempts to do so (Eysenck, 1952). To judge by recent writings, however, there is now less objection to conceiving of the whole self or the whole ego or to studying them by empirical means. In holistic approaches to the study of these hypothetical subsystems, the whole and its parts have been seen as mutually related, changes in a part being capable of affecting the whole and the functioning of the whole being capable of determining what happens in the parts.

This approach stands in sharp contrast to that of the behavior theorist, who puts his faith in methods that make precision of measurement possible and all of whose concepts are in theory readily referred to observable events. The behavior theorist believes that when he proceeds in this way the study of simple processes will eventually lead to the development of a set of empirical laws that will hold for, and permit the understanding of, more complex processes. The dynamic-organismic theorist doubts this. He assumes that personality processes are organized on various levels and that simple processes are always in part determined by the larger organismic patterns and purposes within which they have a place.

Holism was the core principle in the views of Lecky (1945), one of the early important contributors to the theory of the phenomenal self. "The point is that all of an individual's ideas are organized into a single system, whose preservation is essential. In order to be immediately assimilated the idea found as the result of a new experience must be felt to be

consistent with the ideas already present in the system. . . .
The nucleus of the system, around which the rest of the system
revolves, is the individual's idea or conception of himself" (p.
150). Rogers (1959) and other writers more or less identified
with his school of client-centered psychotherapy—Combs and
Snygg (1959), for example—are in Lecky's tradition. Of considerable importance for developments in personality psychology is the fact that Rogers and his students and associates have
not merely adopted holism as a comfortable philosophy but
have made it the cornerstone of their client-centered psychotherapeutic work and research. Regarding the phenomenal self
as the nucleus of personality organization, they argue that the
way to change an individual's behavior is to change his conception of himself. In research on the processes and effects of
psychotherapy or on personality growth, Rogers and his associates explore the phenomenal self directly by a variety of techniques involving self-reports, study diverse patterns of behavior
in relation to the phenomenal self, and see how this self changes
with varying conditions. Since the late 1940s, there has been
an outpouring of research in these areas (for example, Brownfain, 1952; Raimy, 1948; Rogers and Dymond, 1954; Ruben-
stein and Parloff, 1959; Rudikoff, 1954; Seeman and Raskin,
1953). Whereas psychologists differ with respect to their views
of the role and functions of the phenomenal self, not many
deny that such a self exists or that studies of its contents and
vicissitudes are useful.

The behavior theorist (for example, Farber, 1964;
Eysenck, 1959) would argue, however, with the use of some
supporting evidence, that the way to change the self-conception
is to change behavior. Rogers would probably not be upset by
a demonstration that such an effect was achieved, for it is his
view that the whole and its parts are mutually related. He
would ask why the behavior theorist, who presumably is interested in the explanation of all behavior, does not accept the
idea of the determination of a process by the whole in which
it is embedded. The behavior theorist would admit the possibility that a particular behavioral event is influenced by various

processes in the organism but would question how to specify and measure those processes. He would argue that until this specification and measurement become possible, through the slow and deliberate advance of empirical science, better stick to studying the effects of external stimuli, venturing into the vast complexity of the inner processes of the organism only when this can be done without loss of precision of measurement or elegance of theory.

This division among theorists is deep, pervasive, and persistent; it has many implications, as we shall see, but here we are concerned only with the way it influences the psychologist's search for elements. Consider, for example, the matter of size of analytic categories. One may suppose that the choice here depends solely upon the kind of problem the investigator is addressing himself to: that he selects small categories if he is interested in the effects of a visual stimulus and larger categories if he is interested in the effects of a college education. One may suppose, too, that investigators who use small categories are interested in what they may add up to and that those who use large categories are concerned that they lend themselves to analysis into finer units. Generally this is not so. For reasons we have seen, behavior theorists avoid large categories, which rarely seem called for in experimental work, and postpone the task of building their fine and nicely specified units into larger structures. Dynamic-organismic theorists, typically concerned with long sections of behavior and large areas of the person's functioning, do not hesitate to use large categories, such as generalized needs or sentiments. Although admitting the need to understand how such categories are compounded of smaller units, these theorists seem temperamentally disposed to neglect this problem in favor of finding out how a large category fits into a still larger one, such as the ego or the self, and how those major systems relate to the whole personality.

Again, the differing points of view described here are expressed in the degrees of freedom with which theorists use hypothetical constructs. As indicated above, to speak of personality at all is to speak in terms of such constructs. And all

theorists agree that it must be possible to connect the construct
with observable events. The question is how close the connection must be. Behavior theorists introduce hypothetical constructs but are reluctant to enlarge or complicate them. They
insist upon the most direct ties between the constructs and
observable behavior. This insistence has led some of them to
regard personality as nothing more than an aggregate of measurable performances. Dynamic-organismic theorists, on the
other hand, interested in probing the deeper or more central
aspects of the person, often use constructs, such as unconscious
motive, which have only highly indirect ties to anything observable. Theorists of this group are continuing to make free
use of hypothetical constructs but under pressure from their
more cautious colleagues have become increasingly concerned
about the verification of these concepts and have become increasingly sophisticated in respect to the methods by which
this verification is to be accomplished. Klein (1951, 1956, 1962),
for example, works with a psychoanalytic conception of ego
and, armed with a great deal of research, has been a particularly
effective spokesman for holism. "Our target is a theory which
would lead to laws of perceivers, not laws of perception, a
theory which would be not so much concerned with linking
generalized field conditions or states of motivation to perception in general as with linking them with the organization of
people. . . . The placating formula which a person develops
—his equilibrating mechanisms—are his ego-control system.
. . . If analyses of perception are to have any relevance to
personality theory, they must disclose how the control principles, the equilibrating mechanisms, appear in and through
its functioning" (1951, pp. 328–330). Hilgard (1949) has written that "all the [Freudian] mechanisms imply a self-reference,
and . . . the mechanisms are not understandable unless we
adopt a concept of the self" (p. 376).

Although most of these ideas can be found in the works
of the older holistic, or organismic, writers (G. W. Allport,
1955; Goldstein, 1939; Lecky, 1945; Ritter, 1919; Smuts, 1926;
Wheeler, 1940), this general orientation has gained increas-

ingly wide acceptance and is playing an increasingly important role in the design of research as part of a larger trend toward increasing acceptance and utilization of ideas from gestalt psychology (Kofka, 1935; Kohler, 1929; Lewin, 1935), the organismic view in biology (Ritter, 1919; Russel, 1916), and general-systems theory (F. H. Allport, 1955; Grinker, 1956; Miller, 1955, 1960; von Bertalanffy, 1950, 1951). Allport (1937b) remarked that certain conceptions drawn from gestalt psychology (such as Wertheimer's radix, Kofka's ego systems, and Lewin's regions, tension systems, and inner-personal strata) were helpful. MacKinnon (1944) called for an integration of Lewin's topological psychology and the kind of dynamic psychology represented by Murray. And according to Hall and Lindzey (1957), Rapaport, when reviewing Werner's *Comparative Psychology of Mental Development* (1948) in 1940, pointed out that this systematic treatment of development from the gestalt point of view was of great value and that what was needed for an adequate theory of development was an integration of gestalt psychology and psychoanalysis.

Despite a steady increase in the use of gestalt and systems-theoretical concepts by most writers, we are still waiting for an over-all synthesis embodying both a more or less complete gestalt or systems theory and a thoroughgoing functionalist or behavior theory. Sometimes it seems that the concepts have crept into personality theory as they have gradually become a part of the general culture of psychology; sometimes they seem to have been deliberately adopted as a means for supplementing an existing theoretical structure. The quotation from Schjelderup with which we began is an example of the latter case. The gestalt or general-systems concepts are used to build a kind of formal model of the personality (the parts or regions then being filled in with specific contents), and the whole system is set in motion with the use of the psychoanalytic mechanisms.

For a long time the common reaction of American researchers to the gestalt and general-systems imports was that there was nothing wrong with the new concepts except the lack of ways to measure them—nothing wrong, in other words, except that they were useless. However, as abstracted features of the whole personality (integration, adaptability) and the properties of subsystems (breadth, complexity, rigidity, isolation) have become household words among researchers, there has been increasingly wide recognition that one has to have objective indexes for them. Accordingly, researchers have been getting down to the serious business of supplying operational definitions, and these contributions have led to a great increase in the number and variety of personality variables treated in research reports.

If personality is more of a whole than it used to be, it also is more "social." As we have seen, the major accent of the traditional functionalists was on the strivings of the organism rather than on its responsiveness to the environmental stimuli of that moment. To clinch the argument for strivings, the usual recourse was to biology, to man's kinship, at least in this respect, with the lower animals. Freud and McDougall, who were in the tradition of Darwin, must have recognized that the needs to survive and to perpetuate the species were fundamental to all human activity. More modern psychologists, aware of their own purposes, have examined the rat to see whether it is governed in the same way, and this agreeable creature has obliged by confirming most of the hypotheses of purposivism. Meanwhile, however, with the development of anthropology and sociology, evidence has gradually accumulated and has become rather overwhelming that virtually all the distinguishable features of personality are correlated with features of the cultural or social environment of the individual now or in his past. Thus one of the major problems among the personality psychologists of the functionalist point of view has been how to become more "social" without really changing. They are able to point out that their system has always made place for learning in the social environment. Since 1945, however, psychologists have increasingly used a variety of personality variables to represent what has been learned or internalized through interaction with the social environment.

Such variables include role dispositions, interpersonal reaction systems, and social values (Levinson, 1959; Maccoby, 1966; Newcomb, 1950a, 1950b).

A final trend in theory-making may be noted. In the 1930s the personality theorist went to considerable pains to marshal the arguments and the evidence in favor of the generality of his major personality variables (the traits or needs or attitudes that were his units of analysis). For example, Allport (1937b) agreed that honesty was a general trait in the sense that honest behavior was evoked by a wide variety of situations, and Murray (1938) agreed that needs were general in the sense that directed striving was evoked by a kind of stimulus situation and persisted—with variations in instrumental behavior—until a kind of end situation was reached. At the time, personality theorists had to defend such conceptions against the prevalent habit psychology, which argued that particular responses were learned in particular situations and that specific stimulus-response connections were the essential elements of personality (Hartshorne and May, 1928, 1930). The controversy was a lively one for a number of years but has now receded into the background—though it may be becoming salient again (Burwen and Campbell, 1957; Kenny and Ginsberg, 1958). This instance would appear to be one in which a problem more or less disappears, not because it is solved but because it is replaced by other more pressing problems. At any rate, almost all the elements of personality considered in this essay have been conceived as having some generality. Undoubtedly, enough evidence from research has been accumulated so that the authors or defenders of generalized traits, needs, attitudes, or systems feel some security. Yet no one probably would care to argue that specificity of habit or of fixation does not also exist in nature. And the processes of generalization or fixation are just about as obscure as ever. Most students of personality are willing to consider that man is both a generalizing and a fixating animal and that how much generality or specificity characterizes a given disposition of a person is an empirical question.

So far I have sought to show that the kinds of elements in which personality is analyzed proceed from the general theories with which different writers approach the field and that the theories in turn are related to preferences for the method of approach and the problems set. We have already seen that practical problems, such as personality assessment or the development of useful tests, require a minimum of theory and use theoretically neutral elements and categories at once coarser and less abstract than those appealing to the experimentalist or to the devotee of elegant theory. For example, the psychotherapist, faced with vast quantities of verbal material, has no alternative but to employ gross units of analysis; and required to take action, often on short notice, he has to deal with the relatively concrete and particular—without stopping to translate his thoughts into the terms of a general theoretical system. Much the same considerations hold in the case of a psychologist who wishes to develop a test that predicts behavior in some practical situation.

Psychologists who prefer different sizes of analytic categories or levels of abstraction often seem to assume too hastily that they necessarily also differ in fundamental theory or orientation. Thus communication among workers having these different preferences increases very slowly—if at all. One cannot, of course, ask the practical worker to use finer categories or less concrete conceptions than are suited to his purpose; one can ask only that he use concepts that lend themselves to analysis and systematic treatment. And one can ask the general theorist, as he clears up fine points of his scheme by experimentation, to consider occasionally how his fine units may appear in molar behavior and how his general scheme may be filled in with contents familiar to the practical worker.

Related to molarity of elements and abstractness of concepts is the observability of the variables of personality. Strictly speaking, no element of personality is directly observable; all are inferred from behavioral indexes, some more directly than others (Bergmann, 1953; Bergmann and Spence, 1951; Meehl and MacCorquodale, 1948). Some students of personality prefer to stick close to the facts of observation and to treat manifest behavior characteristics as the elements of personality; others permit themselves the use of hypothetical constructs, such as unconscious hostility toward one's father, which have highly indirect ties to what is observable.

The issue involved here has a long history. The early psychology of personality, particularly aspects stemming from the clinic, made free and sometimes freewheeling use of hypothetical constructs. For many critics, this was mysticism and had no place in scientific psychology, which at the time was mainly a know-nothing behaviorism whose stock in trade was objectivity. To these critics of personality theory, the discovery of Bridgman's (1927) operationism was a great boon. It became something of a fashion to reject—as being outside of science—concepts that could not be defined operationally, that is, in terms of steps taken to obtain an objective index of a given concept. It had always been possible to stall a conversation with a personality theorist by asking him to define his terms; now, by asking him to define his terms operationally, one could make him wish he had never spoken. But the personality theorists, exhibiting that adaptability according to which people may change while remaining essentially the same, continued to do what they were doing but more cautiously and with more attention to conceptual clarity and to objective indicators of their hypothetical constructs and theoretical statements.

The personality theorists have been vindicated to a considerable extent. Today it is possible to say that operationism in psychology has changed, while the constructs that came under its strongest attack are very much alive and kicking. A great deal of discussion—led often by philosophers of science (Bergmann, 1953, 1957; Feigl, 1945; Feigl and Brodbeck, 1953; Feigl and Sellers, 1949; Hempel, 1954; Scriven, 1956)—has led to the widely accepted conclusions that the radical operationism of Bridgman is not the best guide in psychological theory-making, that almost no theoretical statements can be completely and directly verified by observation, and that hypothetical constructs not only are necessary to the activity of the human intellect but have brought the best success in predicting and explaining behavior. Modern operationism does not require that every concept be defined in terms of operations but only that it be connectable, however indirectly, with some observable event or process. Thus the operational reformulation of psychoanalysis, as Ellis (1956) has shown, does not involve replacing psychoanalytic concepts and theories with something entirely different—not many of them, at any rate— but involves showing how they may be stated in molar terms at the level of intervening variables so that they may be confirmed or disproved by observation.

Constructs to stand for processes central to or deep within the personality have as good standing as they ever did— perhaps better. But all theorists do not feel free to use such constructs. After all, a bias in favor of the objective, the tangible, and the immediately observable existed long before operationism was invented, as did a bias in favor of the vaguely all-inclusive, the intangible, the difficult to observe, or the unobservable. Psychologists still locate themselves at different places on the scale extending from one of these extreme positions, the objectivist (Gibson, 1959; Skinner, 1950), to the other (Murray, 1959; Rapaport, 1959; Tolman, 1959). And this location is to some extent independent of general theoretical position. A strictly operationalistic psychology is necessarily behavioristic, but modern behaviorists divide rather sharply on the issue of hypothetical constructs. And among personality theorists and clinical psychologists who prefer the vague but inclusive dynamic concepts, some are far more concerned about verifiability than others.

In general, the issue—the free use of hypothetical constructs versus an accent on observability—is not so sharply drawn as it used to be. Although the situation at this moment is somewhat obscure, developments since 1930 show a slow but steady movement toward greater acceptance in personality theory of the less tangible. Psychologists of the more hardheaded variety have discovered that learning from the interesting and dubious conceptualizations of the personologists requires no loss of scientific respectability; but personality and clinical psychologists, whose stock in trade by virtue of their upbringing is the dynamic theories of personality, psychoanalytic or other, have at the same time grown in methodological sophistication.

To some extent, preference respecting elements for the analysis of personality is associated with preference for certain methods of investigation. The psychologist with a strong attachment to the experimental method must, of course, limit himself to appropriate variables. In work on personality, however, certain aspects cannot be experimented upon in the usual laboratory situation—either because of their nature (for example, things apparent only when the person is observed in numerous varied situations or things whose meaning cannot be detected unless they are seen in a very broad context) or because of present technical difficulties or ethical considerations (for example, arousing in a laboratory guilt feelings equal in quality and intensity to those in the clinician's scheme of things).

In these circumstances, the convinced experimentalist is tempted not only to ignore problems for which his method is unsuited but to conceive of personality as made up of elements of the sort that he can get hold of, as it were. Hence he has a tendency to regard personality as an aggregate of measurable performances and to treat measures as elements of personality rather than what they are—dubious indexes of true elements which are also manifested in various other measurable performances. Such method centeredness (Maslow, 1946) naturally makes for superficiality. And it permits the experimentalist to be easier on himself than is healthy. If our gifted experimentalists would spend less time trying to cut personality to fit the pattern of tried and true methodology and more time devising techniques for studying what the dynamic theorist or common sense itself regards as elements of personality, both our experimental methodology and our knowledge of personality functioning would probably advance more rapidly than they currently are. Another example of method centeredness is the tendency, found among experts in objective personality testing by verbal means, to overaccent the consistent and the common to the neglect of the inconsistent and the rare, which may be even more significant. Thus, too, some devotees of projective tests conceive of a personality as an organization of fantasies and defense mechanisms whose overt behavior—difficult to predict from projective tests—does not matter very much. Probably most psychologists would agree, when not forced to defend their favored method, that personality is complicated enough to require study by all existing psychological methods and some that have not yet been invented.

Another preference which makes a difference in the personality elements conceived or preferred is that some students are interested primarily in differences among people, others in differences in the same person through time. In other words, some are interested in durable attributes with respect to which individuals clearly differ, which are predictive of behavior in varied situations, and which provide meaningful and useful bases for sorting people out (Eysenck, 1947; Gough, 1957; Hathaway and McKinley, 1943; Sheldon, 1940); others, in personality change (Christie, 1952; Cowen, Landes, and Schaet, 1959; Macfarlane, Allen, and Honzik, 1954; Sarnoff and Katz, 1954). The investigator of individual differences is likely to concentrate upon attributes (abilities, temperamental traits) or tendencies (introversion-extroversion, neuroticism, delinquency, masculinity-femininity) which are presumed to correlate somehow with the soma or the genes or which on empirical grounds appear to be highly generalized and pervasive. On the other hand, students of change prefer elements which, according to theory, have their major correlates in experience (social attitudes, values, opinions, dispositions in respect to interpersonal relationships). Unlike the inveterate mental tester, though, both experimentalists and psychotherapists are interested in change.

In a survey of psychologists' proposals for elements of

personality, one might naturally assume that the essential or important elements are those most persistently investigated and, similarly, that the psychology of personality can be defined as what personality psychologists do. This game would be a losing one so far as American psychology is concerned, for one's conception of the substance of personality would depend upon the date of the work used as a sample. Thanks to our ability and desire to communicate and our higher regard for facts than for theories, personality research in this country is highly susceptible to trends and fashions. One year values occupy the center of the stage; another year, anxiety or cognitive structures or authoritarianism or the achievement motive. This is not to suggest that the fashionable life is bad —on the contrary, it is interesting and, in a way, productive— but rather that attention to what investigators happen to be doing at a particular time is a poor guide to an understanding of the substance of personality.

The dilemmas confronting the personality theorist today seem in a number of basic ways the same as they were in 1937, but a study of developments since then reveals significant trends in thought and research. Theorists are more aware of each other and frequently more willing to include other people's contributions in their own hopefully comprehensive schemes. This increased awareness has led to an increased sense of the complexity of personality, which manifests itself in repeated calls for a general theory and a cautious modesty about presuming to offer one.

Prominent among personality variables are dynamic elements of the nomothetic order, essential conceptions of the functionalist point of view such as needs, motives, and strivings, with their related goal states, goal objects, and instrumentalities. In recent years, however, motives are being emphasized less and variables of cognition much more. This change is part of a larger movement in the direction of thinking about higher things, a reaction against the biological and clinical emphasis of the older functionalist theories, including psychoanalytic theories. Another part of this movement is the greatly increased interest in the self or ego, part systems of the personality in whose functioning the more highly developed— the more healthy, mature, productive, and efficient—aspects of personality come into their own.

Contemporary holistic, or organismic, thinking about the functioning of the self or of the ego seems part of another general trend—the increasing acceptance and utilization of ideas from gestalt psychology, general-systems theory, and the organismic point of view in biology. The role of these ideas has been not so much to modify existing theoretical schemes as to supplement them; but in performing this function they have led to the conceptualization of numerous new variables of personality (in particular, variables pertaining to the formal properties of subsystems and the whole personality). If personality is more of a whole than it used to be, it is also more social. Developments in sociology and anthropology have been accompanied by a steady increase in the number and variety of personality variables representing what has been learned in the social or cultural environment.

But considerations other than theoretical ones or commitments to particular theoretical systems have influenced the conceptualization of elements of personality. Psychologists concerned with practical problems perforce use categories of analysis that are coarser and less abstract than those which appeal to the experimentalist or devotee of elegant theory. This difference is a continuing source of misunderstanding and failure in communication. Psychologists also differ in the degree of their regard for hypothetical constructs or, more particularly, in their willingness to tolerate indirect or implicit relationships between construct and observable phenomenon. Understanding of the problems involved here has increased greatly in the past twenty years, as psychologists have learned a more sophisticated use of hypothetical constructs.

THREE

Structure
of Personality

The conception of structure is even closer to the heart of a theory of personality than is the choice of elements. One can hardly do justice to the theorists who have attacked this problem without explaining their systems in some detail. In an overview, however, we are required not to summarize a variety of complex systems but rather to set forth a few salient issues and trends. Since there is some affinity between kinds of elements and of organizing principles, we may avoid repetition by merely referring to those theoretical positions already touched upon.

Almost all our definitions of personality mention or

imply organization or patterning of its elements. But there general agreement ends. What does structure of personality mean? The term *structure* refers to all the relationships in personality—to formal relationships (such as inclusion) as well as to functional relationships. Such are not limited to harmonious arrangements or to states of affairs marked by freedom from conflict or inconsistency.

What is structured? It makes a big difference whether we are talking about a life cycle—one conception of personality—or about something that exists for a moment or a relatively short span of time; whether we are talking about the structure of a field that embraces both a person and his actual environment or about a personality that interacts with an environment. Later we discuss these problems of time and of boundaries, but now, in considering general principles, we may regard personality as a more or less stable structure that endures long enough for studies to be made, leaving until later the organization of sequences of changes that occur during an individual's life. Also, we follow most contemporary writers in regarding personality as a system, a set of related variables. This system is no doubt usually a part of some more inclusive system, but this fact does not prevent us from concentrating for the moment upon what F. H. Allport (1955) calls its inside structuring.

The language of personality theory is replete with terms referring to purely formal—as opposed to functional or dynamic—relations among the parts. The earlier quotation from Schjelderup illustrates this point. The use of such terms continues, regardless of whether they are elevated to the status of concepts and regardless of what model of personality functioning one adopts—whether one thinks of personality as being like a machine, a brain, an animal, a building, or a system of a more general sort. In most instances, personality is conceived as existing in space; hence, spatial metaphors are used to describe arrangements of parts and whole. No theorist fails to avail himself of this possibility.

Thus Lewin (1936) began his lectures on personality by

drawing an ellipse on the blackboard to represent the person. The area outside but adjacent to this figure represented the environment. Another ellipse drawn within the first separated the perceptual-motor region, next to the environment, from the inner-personal region, which had no direct contact with the environment. Then by cross-hatching he filled in the inner ellipse to represent regions of the inner-personal sphere, such as needs and habits. He was now in a position to endow these elements of personality and the boundaries separating them with whatever properties his general theory required. Obviously at a given time the regions of personality stood in various purely formal relationships one to another and to the environment. Some regions were connected with many others, some with few. In the inner-personal sphere, some regions were immediately adjacent to the perceptual-motor region and were thus peripheral, representing the more superficial or transitory features of the person. Other regions, in various degrees central or separated from the environment by intervening regions, represented what was deeply important to the person—his self, for example, or needs directly related to it. Boundaries of regions had different degrees of permeability, represented by the width of the boundary lines. For Lewin, personality development involved mainly an increase in differentiation of regions between the self and the environment, and in the impermeability of boundaries separating regions. Fawl (1963) used these conceptions to predict and to find that disturbances are less frequent in older children (whose central regions are better protected from disturbing stimuli) but of longer duration (because the greater impermeability of boundaries makes it more difficult for tension to dissipate).

As we have seen, a great many proposed variables pertain to formal aspects of the whole personality or its parts—to features such as the number of parts and the way they are connected. Other variables pertain to formal relationships among the parts and to their arrangement or distribution with respect to the whole. Thus two or more parts may be related by similarity, proximity, inclusion, and so on; while a given part in its relations to the whole may be described as central (connected with many other parts) or peripheral (isolated), outer (in direct relationship with the environment) or inner.

Although the formal relationships a theorist accents depend to some extent upon the particular model of personality he adopts, these are rarely matters for theoretical dispute. All personality theorists are concerned primarily with dynamic organization, the interaction of processes. They differ mainly on the nature of the processes—the content of the parts or subsystems, as we saw in our consideration of elements—and on the nature of their interaction. Thus everybody agrees that personality is more or less differentiated; but what the differentiated parts are, why and how differentiation occurs—these are matters for some debate. In general, the analysis of personality into states, conditions, arrangements—supposing that these can be observed or more or less accurately inferred—prepares the way for explanation in terms of dynamic theory.

In Lewin's scheme, for example, we first ask which of the regions act upon other regions and what lawful transformations occur in consequence. Personality theorists have, in effect, filled in the regions of Lewin's ellipse with various contents—needs, sentiments, object cathexes, habits, cognitive dispositions—and then developed theory concerning the interactions of these contents and the mechanisms by which effects are achieved. Such theory is used to explain particular formal relationships among particular contents. Lewin himself considered that his formal structures changed readily as a result of dynamic forces. For example, if a person is angry but exercises self-control, the whole inner-personal region becomes more unified (less differentiated, more primitive), while the peripheral regions of the inner-personal sphere become more widely separated from the perceptual-motor region. He allowed, however, that some formal structures persist and may differ from one individual to another.

Certain functional relationships apparently obtain in any operating totality and, like formal relationships, may be regarded as neutral as far as personality theory is concerned.

In machines as well as in organisms, there may be subordination and superordination, means-end relations, or mere coordination (Ashby, 1952). If all theorists are using an operating totality as a model, differences in theory do not become apparent until they begin filling in these abstractions with particular contents. For example, there may be a hierarchy of habits as well as a hierarchy of needs or values.

Personality is universally conceived as a going concern. It is busily adapting itself to forces from outside or initiating activities of its own or both. In any case, energy and information are transferred between the personality and its environment and within the personality. If one concentrates on the personality system by itself, one seeks lawful transactions among the parts and lawful transformations of particular parts.

According to the point of view of functionalism, or action theory, which is traditional and widely accepted among personality theorists, the fundamental organizing principle is striving. Goals are set, and the resources necessary for the attainment of these goals are mobilized. At any moment of a person's existence, at least one need or drive is active, and diverse other processes are being organized in its service. The action point of view permits wide variation in the way the striving itself is conceived. Striving may be induced by a physiological drive and reduce the tension generated by that drive; it may relieve an unpleasant psychological state such as lowered self-esteem or feelings of guilt or may reinstate a condition previously experienced as pleasant; or it may serve some far-flung purpose involving a complicated program of action.

American psychologists have always been hardheaded about teleology, unwilling to attribute events in an organism to final causes, but they have long been more or less generally agreed that directed striving is simply a fact of observation and so can find a place in diverse theoretical systems. As for the why of directed striving, a minimum conception that can be widely accepted is that we strive in order to reduce tension or to restore equilibrium. This notion can be utilized by psychologists who differ widely about how many and which of man's susceptibilities to tension are native and how many are acquired and, for that matter, how many of the acquired ones are merely derivations from the native ones. In stimulus-response psychology, for example, the basic model is provided by the rat running through a maze to get food and thereby to reduce the hunger drive; in psychoanalysis, by the infant seeking and finding the breast and then sucking to get pleasure as well as to relieve his hunger. Other dynamic theories, such as those of McDougall (1923) and Murray (1938), accent more general needs, such as achievement or affiliation, in the service of which the person recalls previous successful strivings, selectively perceives relevant objects and instrumentalities, organizes motor activities, and experiences positive or negative affects depending on the motive that is operating and the progress and ultimate fate of the striving.

With experience, one builds more or less durable structures around motives. Whiting and Child (1953), for example, refer to the behavior system, a set of habits built upon a common drive originating in early childhood; Freud (1943), to character structures (oral, anal); Murray (1938), to the need integrate, a structure embodying a need and the images of objects and the modes of response that have been associated with it; and Murphy (1947), to canalization, the process by which a need becomes directed toward a particular stimulus or class of stimuli.

Psychologists using the disequilibrium-equilibrium formula, whether borrowing the physiological principle of homeostasis (Maze, 1953; Selye, 1946; Stagner, 1951, 1954) or utilizing a formal model, thus differ with respect to the size and complexity of the system or subsystem which they believe exists or is appropriate for analysis. Some prefer to focus upon the tension generated in a particular region of the organism by a particular drive state and reduced by a particular response. Others are more interested in larger systems, such as the ego, which have their own problems of maintaining themselves in a steady state, whatever their origins. All, however, can use the concept of equilibrating mechanisms, the ground in which personality theory flourishes most luxuriantly. Psychologists have produced a great diversity of these mechanisms, ranging all the way from the ego's mechanisms of defense to the conception of tension being reduced by the response to a stimulus. The major theoretical issue here is whether one prefers gestalt principles, such as closure, dynamic self-distribution, and *pragnanz,* or the associationistic principles of behaviorism. Little evidence indicates an early resolution of this issue.

In the view of most writers, personality comprises numerous systems, and theory must take account of their interactions. Obviously, the same system may be viewed with attention to its inside structuring or to its relations with other systems or to the relations of the two. A number of principles of organization have been introduced, such as the means-end relationship, in which immediate goals are means for attaining more distant ones. For Murray (1938), subsidiation is the operation of one need in the service of another. Psychologists widely agree that the classical short section of behavior (exemplified by the rat's successful negotiation of a maze and so intensively studied by experimental psychologists) may have a role in the promotion of long-range objectives. Allport (1961) argues that a motive that develops to further another motive may become functionally autonomous (independent of its origins). For example, a young man who goes to medical school in order to please his father may find in his studies enough satisfaction to sustain an interest in medicine and thus to replace the original motive, which may indeed be forgotten. From the point of view of psychoanalysis the behavior of the young man in this example is overdetermined. If people are going to engage in complex and difficult patterns of activity, it is elementary wisdom to make them serve a multiplicity of needs, including infantile ones. Murray (1938) speaks of a fusion of needs when multiple needs are gratified by a single course of action.

When needs are in conflict, however, a person must somehow choose among them. Psychologists have conceptualized various ways in which this is done. Among them is scheduling (Murray and Kluckhohn, 1955), which permits the attainment of as many goals as possible, one after the other. Again, motivational systems may be simply coordinated, existing side by side, as it were, or one may be a specification or concretization of another. For example, if a person has a generalized attitude of hostility toward a minority group, responses of rejection may be elicited by a great many antiminority items in a test. Another widely used conception is that of hierarchy. In stimulus-response theory, for example, habits are said to be arranged in a hierarchy in the sense that a given stimulus is most likely to evoke some particular response out of several possible ones. This hierarchy holds for the state of affairs both at the time of birth and after experience and learning. Murphy (1947, p. 227) stresses the importance of hierarchies of conditional responses, pointing out that attitudes, which he sees as conditioned responses, determine what responses may later be conditioned. Murray (1951) uses the concept of prepotency to refer to the attribute of a need that leads to its taking precedence over others in a hierarchy. Maslow (1954) has developed this idea more fully. The most prepotent needs are physiological deficiencies, which must be overcome at least to some minimal degree before other needs can operate. Then, in order of prepotency, there are safety needs, belongingness and love needs, esteem needs, and self-actualizing needs.

Despite its central place in traditional personality theory and in much other psychological theory, the tension-reduction hypothesis (the homeostatic principle) has in recent years come in for some hard knocks or well-calculated neglect, at least. With the new emphasis on the normal and the higher, one hears less about the individual's adjustments or adaptations and more about his self-activity and natural growth tendencies. In addition, many psychologists, including some of the more hardheaded ones, have expressed dissatisfaction with the equilibrium formula, especially as the principle underlying all motivation.

Tension reduction is a broader concept than that of drive reduction, in Hull's (1943) original meaning of this term.

In animal psychology a great deal of discussion and experimentation has been directed to the question of whether all striving is in the interest of drive reduction. For Hull all drives were aversive. The counterargument was that at least some drives were appetitive, that striving sought to induce change in the direction of positive affect. The matter has now been more or less settled in favor of the latter position, a major blow being struck by Olds and Milner's (1954) demonstration that animals exhibited goal responses suggesting a strong interest in the affects produced by electrical stimulation of a certain area of the brain. Most personality theorists seem never to have doubted that human beings seek experiences that have given them pleasure in the past, that they go to great lengths to find excitement or have fun, showing signs of tension when gratification is delayed or denied. The successful critique of drive reduction, then, does not settle the issue of tension reduction, which involves the homeostatic principle itself.

Some of the old tension-reduction theories were based on analogies to simple physical systems or certain physiological systems in which the final state of equilibrium was the same as that which existed before the disequilibrating circumstances arose. Now it is frequently pointed out that the final and the initial states of equilibrium are very apt to be different, that organisms grow and develop, and thus the equilibrium they attain must somehow take account of their increased size and complexity. As Bühler (1951) puts it, "The individual tries to maintain equilibrium at the same time that he expands." One could still say that the individual often tries to recapture his earlier states of equilibrium but, the world being what it is, has to change in order to maintain the same level of stability that he enjoyed before. Thus, within limits, the stable states of the individual must be on progressively higher levels. Probably this general view of the matter does not encounter strong objections among personality theorists today.

Another and more controversial criticism is that equilibrium—however new or high its level—is not enough. Bühler (1951), for example, starts with the notion that the basic tendency in life is toward expansion (growth and reproduction) and then argues that homeostatic mechanisms are only one aspect of this larger process. She quotes Cannon on the point that homeostasis frees the organism for more complicated social tasks, and she aligns herself with Goldstein (1939), whose self-actualization is the drive that carries the organism on to activity after equilibrium has been reached. Bühler cites with approval Fenichel's (1945) conception of homeostasis as a process having the aim of maintaining a level of tension that is characteristic for the healthy organism, rather than abolishing tension altogether. This view is in keeping with Goldstein's (1939) notion that the healthy organism maintains a level of tension adequate to enable it to initiate further activity. Thus it is the nature of organisms to raise tension levels that are too low and to lower levels that are too high, from the point of view of the well-being and growth of the organism. Murray and Kluckhohn (1955) list generation of tension among the major functions of personality. Taking issue with Freud, as they say, they argue that what generally most satisfies a healthy organism is not a lack of tension but the process of reducing tension—hence people see to it that they have tensions to reduce. In the same vein, Mowrer (1950) distinguishes what he regards as two fundamentally different learning processes, solution learning and sign learning. "Solution learning is problem-solving, drive-reducing, pleasure-giving; whereas sign learning, or conditioning, is often—perhaps always—*problem-making*" (p. 5; italics mine).

Mowrer's point is reminiscent of Maslow's (1954) distinction between coping behavior and expressive behavior. But here a new conception appears. Not only do organisms or personalities do things in order to further some objective or other —to reduce tension or to raise it, but they also just do things. Murray and Kluckhohn (1955), after calling self-expression a function of a personality, say, "More basic and elementary than integrated goal-directed activities are the somewhat anarchic, uncoordinated medley of tentative, short-lived mental processes which characterize the stream of consciousness during periods of rest and day dreaming, at one extreme, and during periods of intense emotional excitement or lunacy, at the other. For these spontaneous, random, ungoverned, but yet expressive cacophonies of energy we have proposed the term 'process activity.' This is pure Being, a state in which the mind moves in its own inherent manner for its own intrinsic pleasure" (p. 37). These processes do become "shaped into effective or aesthetic patterns—telling gestures, ritual dances, songs, dramas —which are more perfectly expressive of emotion or of valuations." All this, of course, is much like Bühler's (1924) conception of function pleasure.

Murray and Kluckhohn, in the systematic statement from which the above quotation was taken, devote about as much space to process activity and the generation of tension as to the reduction of tension. Again, the critique of drive reduction and the presentation of alternative processes take up a great deal of space in literature on motivation and personality theory, as in Combs and Snygg's (1959) accent on enhancement of the phenomenal field, in the existentialist search for meaning (May, Angel, and Ellenberger, 1958), and in Maslow's (1954) theory of growth motives. Granted that a basic tendency of life is to grow and develop, the question remains, what makes growth occur? What are the mechanisms of developmental change? And what prevents development? The study of college students suggests that it is just as natural for them to remain as they are as it is for them to enhance their phenomenal fields or to seek new levels of order and transaction (Sanford, 1966). Teachers may further student development by finding ways to show that people are not forever bound by their childhood conditioning or by a closed system of social forces and ways to challenge students by upsetting their equilibrium and generating moderate degrees of tension.

Since critics of tension reduction have shown that life consists of more than reducing aversive drives, overcoming deficiencies, coping with anxiety, or being blindly conditioned, and that the personality contains more than seems to have been dreamt of by classical psychoanalysis or contemporary behavior theory, a student unversed in history and inexperienced in the game of trying to induce changes in behavior or personality may easily assume that tension reduction is of no special importance and is, perhaps, on the way out. In fact, this conception is of enormous importance and still very much with us. The tension-reduction hypothesis got personality theory off the ground and made clear to the literate public that scientific psychology meant business. The hypothesis had to be fought for and defended, for it was far less palatable to man thinking about himself than notions like self-expression or self-initiated activity.

Today the central importance of tension reduction is so well established that its proponents can relax. As a result, they are giving attention to certain previously neglected processes or features of the person, and a kind of balance is being restored. Moreover, the criticisms of drive-reduction theory by such writers as McClelland (1955; McClelland and others, 1953), Olds (1955), Koch (1956), Hebb (1949, 1958), and White (1959), in addition to those mentioned above, have made clear the need for a more general theory of human motivation. Among promising efforts in this direction are those of Koch (1956), who distinguishes between intrinsic and extrinsic motivation; those of Mowrer (1960), who stresses the importance of affects in accounting for anticipatory behavior; and particularly those of Tomkins (1961), who regards the affective system as primary (in the sense that affects do not require concurrent amplification from the drive system) and as more general than the drive system (in the sense that affects may be triggered by a greater variety of activators and give rise to a greater variety of behavior). It seems safe to say, however, that the general theory to be evolved will give a place to the idea of tension reduction.

To get away from the tension-reduction formula is, apparently, to take a more optimistic view of man's nature. Theorists who do this prefer processes that are less mechanical, consider that man does more than just adapt, and assume that he has the potential for higher levels of functioning from the beginning. Allport is right in saying that the issue is basically philosophical and that behaviorism and classical psychoanalysis follow the Lockean tradition, putting a minimum into personality at the beginning and accenting the building up.

The Leibnizian tradition has been gaining ground of late. Its advocates sometimes speak of themselves and their work as a third force in psychology. Theorists of this group center attention on the experiencing person, oppose the use of mechanistic models of psychological functioning, accent meaningfulness rather than methodological elegance in the selection of problems, and, in general, are concerned with the dignity and worth of man. In general, these theorists favor the dynamic-organismic approach and oppose behavior theory; they tend to lump psychoanalysis and behaviorism together, as the two other forces. Sometimes, however, a distinction is made between the older psychoanalysis, which is one of the other forces, and psychoanalytic ego psychology, which, in some of its versions at least, seems to qualify as third force. Most of the modifications of classical psychoanalysis that have been wrought on American soil—by Fromm (1947), Horney (1937, 1939), Sullivan (1953), and Szasz (1959), for example—have indicated that personality is from the beginning more organized and able to organize than Freud supposed. Official psychoanalysis itself seems at last to have heard the voice of Leibniz (Gill, 1959; Pumpian-Mindlin, 1959; Rapaport, 1958). The autonomous ego of Hartmann, Kris, and Loewenstein (1947) blesses man from the beginning with organizing powers; he is spared the necessity of deriving them from his id in the interests of survival. This view, of course, brings psychoanalysis into a closer relationship than it has previously had with classical general psychology, according to which mechanisms of perceiving, learning, and thinking are aspects of man's nature. Within the Leibnizian tradition, one group of writers attribute to man's nature that which is potentially high or complicated or good—shades of Rousseau. Matters used to be the other way around. Instincts, with all their capacity for evil, were the major features of man's native endowment; and an optimist was a man who—like Freud and the behaviorists—believed that man could nonetheless learn, however painfully, from his experience and so attain a measure of freedom.

No doubt, this whole issue—with its philosophical roots and ideological foliage—should be seen in the light of history. Such a perspective may reveal that the Lockean tradition opened the way to the scientific study of man's mind and, by its accent on the possibilities of change through experience, prepared the way for the revolutionary changes in social institutions that began in Britain and were even more marked in America and in France. Our American distaste for a pessimistic emphasis on human nature has certainly persisted, as witness the fact that Kleinian psychoanalysis (Klein, 1948), the most potent school of psychoanalytic thought in Britain, does not flourish here. Since the Kleinian brand emphasizes the instinctual nature of aggression and the universality of stages of development, it seems its exclusion stems from this bias. Our hopeful outlook has apparently rendered us unable to resist suggestions about man's native goodness.

On the other hand, remarks about American optimism may be wearing a bit thin. After all, save for the case of Klein, we have found a place for virtually all the European and British trends of psychological thought, and that great "pessimist," Freud, won much greater acceptance in America than among British and Continental psychologists. (At the Salzburg Seminar in American Studies in 1952, I lectured mainly on Freud. This material was new and rather unpalatable to most of the young Continental social scientists.) A quick reading of the symposium on European and American personality theory held at the International Congress of Psychology in Montreal (*Proceedings*, 1954) fails to reveal any mention of Freud by the Continental theorists. No doubt, this neglect has much to do with the virtual absence of clinical psychology in Europe, but even among psychiatrists Freud is more widely accepted in America than in Europe. European-American comparisons —always difficult owing to the diversity in both places—have been rendered almost impossible by the immigration since 1935 of so many of the greatest and most influential European psychologists. If, however, we are to remark on American optimism, we must also note the pessimism which many European intellectuals have long worn like a badge and which is sometimes no more than an inverted romanticism.

Whatever its major geographical locus, the new emphasis on innate human nature has perhaps been carried far enough to restore the balance upset by the surge of behaviorism and psychoanalysis. Man may indeed turn out to be from the beginning more worthy than he appeared from these two points of view. But the great danger of putting too much into the personality at the start is that one may thus dodge the difficulties of looking into origins. Stimulus-response psychology may have erred in giving man so few native endowments, but at least it has faced up to the task of explaining how personality builds up.

Of course, the present excursion into the sociology of knowledge should not be permitted to obscure the fact that the nature-nurture question is still fundamentally an empirical one. Ideology flourishes in the absence of solid fact about man's native endowments. Developments in neurophysiological and biopsychological knowledge have been favorable to the more optimistic of the positions described above. Current models of the nervous system (Ashby, 1952) are far more differentiated than those employed by classical stimulus-response psychology, and we have evidence that man comes into the world with more complex capacities than was commonly supposed even in the 1940s (Granit, 1955; Penfield, 1955; Penfield and Jasper, 1954). This evidence, however, does not diminish the importance of learning or of the early development of personality. Rather, it suggests that learning is a more subtle and complicated business than it is often taken to be and that a fresh approach to learning in the framework of the new neurophysiological models may permit us to come to grips with the complexity of personality at last.

If behaviorism and psychoanalysis put little into the personality to begin with and concentrate on what is built up, another school of thought says the personality never does contain very much as far as organization is concerned. According to this point of view, a great deal (perhaps most) of the consistency and order that we observe in behavior is to be attributed to regularities in the social and cultural environment in which the behavior is occurring. Starting with the indisputable fact that all behavior depends upon the individual's situation (the constellation of environmental stimuli, usually social) as well as upon factors within him, the situationist chooses to accent the former, seeking the correlates of behavior in such situational factors as the individual's group memberships or social role. Typically he places or observes many individuals in a given situation and notes the similarities in their responses. These are major (and, of course, legitimate) concerns of social psychology. What makes the personality psychologist anxious is the inclination of some social psychologists (for example, Cantril, 1947; Sherif and Cantril, 1947) to overaccent the presumed similarities among all people and to suppose that the universal human endowment consists mainly of a few dispositions—to imitate social norms, to conform with the requirements of social roles, and the like—which make people adapt to their society and culture. Society and culture thus become the sovereign organizers of human behavior and human life, and the personality psychologist is left with nothing to do.

Field theory, in the hands of many of its adherents, often adds up to about the same thing. Lewin's (1935) field theory started out as a purely psychological theory. Behavior was to be understood as a result of the interplay among factors in the person and in the psychological environment. But much of the experimental work in this tradition has tended to smudge the boundaries between the psychological and the objective (or nonpsychological) environments or to proceed as if the relations between them were one to one. In addition, since factors in the objective environment are much easier to get hold of than those in the person, the experimental work has tended to accent the former and neglect the latter, sometimes even reducing the person to a point region. In field theory, it is the field that is organized—and if the field is comprised over-whelmingly of environmental forces, what place is left for a psychology of personality?

In addition, some psychologists argue or imply that the personality, as it has been traditionally conceived, is not a suitable unit for psychological study; since the individual is always enmeshed in a network of interrelationships with other individuals and since nothing about his behavior can be fully understood apart from this context, one should focus not on relationships within an individual (his organization) but on interpersonal relationships (Sullivan, 1953); not on the monadic unit as Sears (1951a) calls the single individual, but on dyadic units (aggregations of two or more individuals).

These developments have not caught the traditional personality psychologist unprepared. His answer to the situationist has been somewhat as follows: "You are interested in situations; I am interested in persons. You are interested in behavior per se; I am interested in behavior because it is the only means I have for finding out about the dispositions of people and about how they are organized. You proceed by subjecting many individuals to the same situation and noting the communalities in their responses; I proceed by observing the same individual in a variety of situations and noting his persistent tendencies." The answer to the field theorists in the tradition of Lewin has been less sharp. As pointed out earlier, personality theorists of the functionalist, or action, orientation have been generally receptive to topological gestalt psychology; they have addressed themselves to the Lewinian experimentalists in terms more of sorrow than of reproach. "It is too bad that you seem unable or unwilling to conceive and to measure variables in the person or to put a little content into the regions and systems which you suppose to exist there. If you did, your understanding of people would be deeper and your predictions of behavior more accurate."

Preference for certain units of analysis is, of course, an arbitrary matter that need not involve theoretical controversy. If a personality theorist complains that Sullivan's or Sears's units are too large, he must be prepared for the same complaint from psychologists who believe that subsystems—needs or habits, for example—are about as large as anyone can hope to investigate thoroughly. Still—if only for sentimental reasons—some people will probably always want to focus on the individual himself, rather than on some of his parts or the social systems of which he is a unit. Since man the individual—not groups or psychical subsystems—knows joy and suffering and bears moral responsibility, he will probably always be the object of a certain amount of sympathetic curiosity.

Of course, a focusing on a given unit of analysis is likely to have some basis in theory, and this seems to be the case with Sullivan and Sears. In Sullivan's view, the person—the other person—is the most important source of stimuli for the developing individual. Sullivan's exclusion of stimuli arising in certain zones of the body (accented in Freudian psychoanalysis) and those arising in the part objects (for example, the breast, accented in Kleinian psychoanalysis) appears to be quite arbitrary. However, in the present state of our knowledge, such choices of what to emphasize and what to leave out are not only possible but actually necessary to successful theory-making. Sears (1951a) is primarily interested in predicting overt behavior. In proposing the dyadic unit, he takes the position of the social psychologist, whose concern is with all the correlates of a given kind of behavior. Undoubtedly one may hope to account for more of the variance in the aggressive behavior of children by assessing variables not only in them but in the people to whom they are close. Such investigations are all very well, but they are not a particular concern of the student of personality.

Although the personality theorist may have answers for the situationist and the cultural determinist, he has been influenced by them through the years. Personality psychology has become more social not only with respect to elements but also with respect to the locus of organizing principles. Increasingly we realize that we do not detract from such favorite concepts as the superego, ego identity, or self-concept by supposing that

—despite their relative stability and autonomy—they are to some degree sustained as well as formed by forces in the social environment and may be altered radically by extreme social change. Indeed, such realization has been furthered by certain observations of how shifts in the pattern of the individual's social environment may penetrate effectively his deeper or more central regions. For example, Bettelheim's (1943) observations of life in a German concentration camp show that the ego and the self-concept were radically transformed when the individual was removed from his sustaining normal environment to a setting in which he and his fellows were systematically treated as cruel and capricious parents would treat a child. Again, my study of the University of California loyalty oath controversy (Sanford, 1953) concluded that the ego identity of the professor depended heavily upon his role and status, that the integrated functioning of his conscience depended on the support of his colleagues and community, and that his superego could be changed—in the direction of narrowness and externalization—through his acceptance of an imposed loyalty oath. That central structures of the personality are still being formed by the social environment when the individual reaches late adolescence is attested to by studies of college students carried out during the past fifteen years. I have elsewhere (Sanford, 1962) attempted to summarize much of this work under the headings freeing of impulse (changes in the relations of the id to the ego and the superego), enlightenment of conscience (absorption of the superego by the ego), and differentiation and integration of the ego.

This line of thought has suggested some interesting hypotheses. For example, Werner (1948) has proposed that the degree of differentiation of personalities in a society depends on the degree of functional differentiation in that society. If there are few functions to be performed, few roles to be taken, and little possibility of varying performances within these roles, and if there are culture patterns to provide satisfaction for basic emotional needs, then an individual has little reason to develop a wide range of higher psychological needs and modes of coping, which then have to be integrated within the personality. The extreme case is that of a society so undifferentiated that the individual has no conception of himself apart from his family and tribe.

The idea that the more structure or integration there is in a culture the less internal integration an individual needs or can develop has also been suggested by studies of authoritarianism in the United States and in Arab nations (Prothro and Melikian, 1953; Sanford, 1957). Arab students scored significantly higher than American students on the California F scale but did not show in their everyday behavior the rigidity and compulsiveness which, on the basis of studies in the United States, have been commonly associated with authoritarian personality trends. Because a high proportion of the sentiments expressed in the F scale were traditional in Arab culture, individuals could obtain relatively high scores on authoritarianism merely by accepting cultural norms. Adorno and his colleagues (1950) argue that authoritarianism serves important functions for the personality; for example, it provides a means for organizing experience and a way of managing sexual and aggressive impulses. Thus, if the culture itself largely takes care of these functions and is at the same time highly integrated, the individual does not have to develop his own means for performing them.

This way of looking at the individual in relation to social structure appears to be highly relevant to the study of the effects of technological change upon personality (Sanford, 1970). For example, productive organizations in our society define their roles more and more narrowly at the same time that they provide a total environment for the individual who occupies a given role; they may provide security, identity, status, and group solidarity at the same time that they meet purely economic needs. After an employee has been with a company for a while, his internal systems come to depend for their equilibrium upon the systems of the organization itself; a split within the higher councils of the organization, for example, can now affect the individual in much the way he was affected by a quarrel between his parents when he was a child. Men who occupy executive or administrative positions in such organizations often perceive a conflict between what they feel they ought to do and what it seems they must do in order to conform with a policy of the organization. The conflict is often resolved by going along with the team; in other words, by replacing conscience with the ways of a group, with consequent loss in individuality.

It is a familiar idea from Marx that those of us who live in industrial societies are shaped and processed in accord with the demands of productive operations. This molding occurs not only in industry but in classrooms, where we segregate people by age, sex, intelligence, and even personality, so that all in a given class can be taught by a particular teaching device and the teacher is spared having to adjust his activities to the needs of the individual student. In recent years various writers—for example, Wilson (1969)—have been pointing out that virtues such as reliability, punctuality, and frugality, which characterize the good worker in industrial societies, are becoming irrelevant in the present postindustrial society of the United States. In psychodynamic terms, the content of the superego is changing, and the fact that the change is more marked in the younger than in the older generation is an important reason for the current generation gap.

It is common nowadays to speak of the United States as a consumer society and to suggest, with Marcuse (1964), that not only our work but our play, our ways of enjoying life, are shaped by technology. In order to keep the wheels of industry turning advertising and propaganda urge us to do our duty as good consumers. If choice with respect to quality becomes less, never mind, for we can make up for that in the quantity of our consumption. If nothing were done through education to counter the natural trend of technology, we could become, in our personality structure, as simple as—but less human than —members of a preliterate society.

Clearly, at this stage in the development of personality psychology, nothing is to be gained by opposing personality factors and the social system and asking which is the more important. Nor is anything to be gained by conceiving global constellations of field forces in which the individual is somehow enmeshed. What is needed is more knowledge of the articulation of personality systems and social systems. For example, it hardly suffices merely to say, as many social scientists do, that the peron assimilates the culture and that personality is essentially a carrier of culture patterns. Is the cultural element incorporated by the personality a faithful reflection of what exists outside? Or does assimilation involve a person-culture interaction, the addition to the individual's psychological household being a product of something from the culture and something that was already there in the person? To what subsystem of the person is the cultural element assimilated? From a psychodynamic point of view it would make a big difference, both to the individual's development and to the functioning of the groups of which he was a member, whether the element became a part of the superego or a part of the ego. If the former, then the cultural element—a particular value, let us say—would come under the sway of the superego's characteristic modes of functioning and would, therefore, express itself in a somewhat nonrational and unpredictable way, remain dependent upon external reinforcement, and be susceptible to replacement by a different—or even contrary—value when this change was urged by a social group. If, on the other hand, the value were assimilated by the ego, it would become meaningfully related to other values, would be brought into the service of the individual's larger purposes, would gain the support of the need to maintain self-respect, and thus would become an integral and durable feature of the personality. It appears also that cultural elements are assimilated to the superego and to the ego by different processes—to the former most commonly by identification, imitation, and simple conditioning, to the latter most commonly through understanding and reasoning.

Thus, an understanding of the relations of the individual and the social group requires more rather than less attention to the relatively autonomous personality structures and requires searching analysis of social structures in psychologically relevant terms. The student of personality will still focus primarily upon the internal structuring of personality, but he will realize that his hypothetical subsystems are not fully understandable unless the social conditions of their change can be specified.

Freud remains the greatest contributor to the dynamic psychology of personality. Although various conceptions of dynamic structure have been developed as alternatives to Freudian concepts or are concerned with areas of personality neglected by Freud, a discussion of these matters must be introduced by a brief examination of Freud's major ideas. His theory of the plasticity of motives is still basic to contemporary psychodynamic views. This theory is probably as elegant as any in psychology, in that it uses only a few simple principles in explaining a wide range of different and seemingly meaningless phenomena: dreams, slips of the tongue, neurotic symptoms. Freud amassed much evidence to show the importance of sexual (that is, erotic or libidinal) drives and of aggressive drives in the functioning of personality. These drives, typically, are directed toward other people and therefore become the objects of social control, which is possible because of their plasticity. Capable of being satisfied in various ways and with the use of various objects, these drives lend themselves to patterning in more or less socially acceptable ways. But this social acceptability is not achieved without a struggle. Drives tend to persist in their original form after the child has attached himself to his parents and learned to speak to himself as they would speak. The stage is thus set for inner conflict—and for the elaboration of personality structures—as the individual generates highly complex arrangements in order to avoid anxiety or to ward off external punishment while at the same time obtaining gratification of basic needs.

The most distinctive feature of psychoanalytic knowledge is the idea that things are not always what they appear to be and may indeed mean the opposite of what they seem to mean, that meaning is to be searched for in the ways in which the underlying sexual and aggressive needs have been transformed. This transformation is rarely if ever complete, for infantile needs are often rendered unconscious as a means of avoiding the anxiety occasioned by a conflict between some sexual or aggressive drive on the one hand and the internalized version of the restraining forces of society (the superego) on the other. Content made unconscious is henceforth unaltered by experience but persists by its own laws, meanwhile affecting the conscious. Freud and his followers produced many theoretical notions to explain how unconscious processes are reflected in consciousness or are transformed or are disguised in such a way as to make them compatible with conscious aspirations, and how the more conscious, controlling systems of personality ward off, defend themselves against, manage, or integrate unconscious processes. This is the theory to explain dreams, jokes, slips, and symptoms; it is also designed to explain the persistence into adult life of childish ways and constructions, which are capable of dominating the individual's behavior in critical situations.

Whereas id and superego processes are automatic, inflexible, and repetitive in disregard of consequences, other needs are likely to be conscious and to have the benefits of the individual's most highly developed abilities. To account for these last Freud (1927) introduced the concept of ego. It makes a great difference, in psychoanalytic theory, whether a need, with its integrated images and affects, is in the ego or under the sway of the id or superego. In the ego are such structures as rational plans for action, sustained strivings to carry out promises or to uphold principles, and highly differentiated preferences. "Where id was there shall ego be," Freud said, thus implying that personality develops toward the integration and the domination of the whole by ego processes. This state can be represented according to Lewin's scheme as many well-differentiated regions, with flexible boundaries permitting maximum intercommunication.

Freud, during most of his life, considered that the ego was generated out of conflict between the drives and the social forces (or their internal representatives). He was never very clear about this theory, nor have many of his psychoanalytic followers been altogether happy with it. The theory left psychoanalysis open to the criticism that it explained the element of fixity in personality far better than it explained change or development and that it failed to account for man's highest, most complicated, and most constructive activities. In 1939 Hartmann (1958) argued that if psychoanalysis was to be a general psychology of development, it would be necessary to posit ego development outside the sphere of conflict. He proposed that apparatuses of the ego—the beginnings of abilities such as perception, memory, and inhibition—were independent of the drives at birth and developed under the impact of external stimuli, independent of determinants in the drive system (id) and of conflicts between id and ego. Hartmann argued not only for this primary autonomy but also, like G. W. Allport (1955), for the idea that ego activities, though they have their beginnings in the id or in id-ego conflicts, can become functionally independent of their origins, achieving secondary autonomy.

In this effort to develop a psychoanalytic ego psychology, Hartmann was joined by a number of psychoanalysts—for example, Kris and Loewenstein (Hartmann, Kris, and Loewenstein, 1947), Pumpian-Mindlin (1959), and Gill and Brenman (1959)—and by some psychologists friendly to psychoanalysis— for example, Rapaport (1958) and White (1963a). Thus psychoanalysis has tended to come closer to academic psychology. For example, psychologists have conceptualized many phenomena which ego psychology now seeks to explain as parts of the self—something about which Freud had little to say. Thus Lecky (1945) argues that the individual's conception of himself is the nucleus of a system into which all his ideas are organized and with which new experiences have to seem consistent, or at least unthreatening, in order to be assimilated. Rogers (1959) and Combs and Snygg (1959) regard the phenomenal self as the core of the personality organization and have studied by empirical methods the dimensions of the self, the ways in which patterns of behavior are related to it, and the conditions under which it changes. Hilgard (1949) holds that the functioning of a wide range of motivational systems, including the Freudian mechanisms of defense, depends upon the activities and states of the inferred self—a structure underlying the self of awareness. Allport (1943) hails the development of ego psychology as a sign that psychoanalytic writers are at last ready to pay some attention to man's higher achievements.

For most psychologists, it would seem, psychoanalytic ego psychology attends to matters that have always fallen within the general domain of psychological inquiry. What is psychoanalytic about the new ego psychology? Does it build any important bridges between psychoanalysis and the rest of psychology? In spite of some agreement to seek agreement and many fresh observations of ego-functioning, a true integration of psychoanalysis and academic psychology is far from being achieved.

Loevinger (1965, 1966) cogently argues that rather than positing an ego autonomous from the beginning, we should try to explain ego development with the same principles used to explain other phenomena of psychoanalysis. Loevinger proposes that Freud's idea of mastery through reversal of voice be used to supply a dynamic basis for ego development. Freud had concluded that his pleasure principle was not adequate to explain such phenomena as the repetitive play of children and the apparent need of people to relive traumatic experiences. Underlying this compulsion to repeat must be a need to master problems by repeating actively what one has experienced passively—as in identification with an aggressor—and also by reliving in the passive role experiences in which one had been active. Loevinger argues that this principle is at the core of the ego's functioning and is the governing principle in the initial separation of the ego from impulse.

Writers on psychoanalysis continue to debate whether an account of ego development requires entirely new, non-psychoanalytic principles, such as a need for mastery (Hendrick,

1942) or independent ego energies (White, 1963a). For psycho-analysis this question is of crucial importance, for it is basic to the larger question of whether psychoanalytic theory can become a general theory of personality development and functioning.

If it does, then unconscious processes will have to be integrated into such a theory. Few, if any, personality theorists today appear to believe that a person is aware of all the processes determining his behavior at any particular time. Murray and Kluckhohn (1955) propose using the adjective *regnant* for "the momentarily governing processes at the superordinate level of integration in the brain field" (p. 7). Conscious processes are regnant, but not all regnant processes are conscious. More familiar is the notion of James (1890) that whereas we are fully conscious of activities we are in the process of learning, activities that have become habitual tend to recede from our awareness. Linton (1945) elaborates and clarifies this point. He distinguishes between emergent and established responses; the former grade into the latter, but the polar positions in the series seem clear enough.

At the emergent end of the scale we have those behaviors which are evoked by new and unfamiliar situations. . . . At the established end of the scale we have those behaviors which are evoked by familiar situations. Such behaviors are thoroughly organized and patterned. While the emergent responses always involve some degree of consciousness of the situation and of effort to solve the problem which it presents, established responses are automatic and can be produced without either the registry of the situation or the associated behavior attaining a conscious level.

The responses which any individual is capable of making extend over the full range represented by this scale, but their distribution in the scale is far from uniform. . . . It is easier to live by habit than by conscious intent, and most of us do live by habit most of the time. . . . The fact that we can carry on most of our activities at the habitual level serves to conserve

*energy and to provide the surplus vigor required to develop
new forms of behavior as the need for them arises. . . . We
may picture the personality as consisting of an organized relatively persistent core of habits surrounded by a fluid zone of
behavioral responses which are in process of reduction to
habitual terms. [pp. 93–95]*

Processes may be conscious or unconscious, then, depending upon the situation and needs of the organism. They
are likely to be unconscious if there is no need for their conscious activity, if other processes occupy the center of the stage,
or if their being unconscious is favorable to the economy of
the over-all functioning of the organism. But presumably such
processes are capable of becoming conscious if a new situation
requires that they be reviewed. They are not forcibly prevented
from becoming conscious by the operation of other factors in
the personality. Processes which are so barred from access to
awareness are unconscious in Freud's (1938) original meaning
of this term. It is the unconscious in this sense which plays the
crucial role in the psychoanalytic theory of neurosis and is the
cornerstone of the dynamic theory of personality favored by
many clinical psychologists today.

According to action theory, processes are made unconscious or are debarred from consciousness to serve some need—
usually a rather intense need—of the personality (to resolve a
conflict, to reduce anxiety, to preserve self-esteem, to remove
a sense of threat to the integrity of the personality). The repression of psychological contents and the maintenance of bar-
riers to their again becoming conscious are thus adaptive
strategems or mechanisms—adaptive, however, only in some
limited or temporary way, for, as we have seen, consciousness
itself is unquestionably the highest adaptive power of the personality. Repression is a reaction to crisis; it occurs when strains
upon the personality are greater than can be managed by the
more differentiated, the more refined and elegant, the more
flexible—all of which is to say, the more conscious—systems
that have developed. Repression is a function both of the in-

tensity of the strain and of the adequacy of the conscious systems. In childhood, the conscious controlling systems are weak —relative to those in adulthood—and strains are as great as at any time; hence childhood is preeminently the time for repression.

Unfortunately, adaptations made under conditions of extreme strain cannot be easily reversed, particularly if, as is so often the case, strains are continuing. Adaptations resorted to in the face of one strain are probably generalized to others. The personality, meanwhile, keeps growing—not just by undoing its early adaptations, but by incorporating them into its larger structures. The early primitive adaptations remain like wounds in the trunk of the tree; though they may be to some extent encapsulated, all future growth must go around them. More than this, as old wounds, they are susceptible to reopening or disease.

One need not seek far for the implications for personality organization. Unconscious structures have their own distinctive response characteristics and their own laws of functioning (Kubie, 1954; Miller, 1951). They are related dynamically to the conscious processes of the personality. Indeed, a vast amount of personality theory, particularly that which is influenced by Freudian psychoanalysis, is taken up with just this matter. According to the theory by which personality is organized in levels, nowadays called stratification theory, the place of the unconscious is a highly complicated matter. Personality theorists have long spoken of unconscious processes as being on a deeper level than conscious ones. In his early work, Freud divided the psyche into the conscious, the preconscious, and the unconscious, a topography that has not been challenged in psychoanalytic thinking. It has commonly been considered that the unconscious was at the deepest level, the conscious at the most superficial. In more recent personality theory, however, the surface-depth dimension has been conceived in quite different ways. I have attempted to summarize the major trends of thought on this problem (Sanford, 1956a), noting that the adjective *deeper* has been used in diverse ways

—to refer to processes less available to consciousness or to the motoric; to processes laid down earlier in the individual's development; to biological as opposed to learned responses; to the neurologically lower; to the determining or ruling rather than to the determined or ruled or instrumental; to processes that are inner in the sense of not being dependent upon immediate field conditions; to processes that are relatively resistant to change; and finally, to processes that are relatively hidden from observation. Each of these conceptions is accompanied by theory concerning the determinants of relationships between processes on the deeper levels and processes on more superficial ones. Processes that are unconscious in Freud's sense may have any or all of the characteristics just listed, but none of these characteristics applies only to such unconscious processes. These processes have to be distinguished by their own special dynamics, a matter that has been the chief concern of a vast quantity of psychoanalytic observation and theory. Unconscious motives are commonly said to be marked primarily by insatiability, by resistance to modification through experience, and by lack of response to pleasure or pain, rewards or punishments, logic or argument. Behavior that proceeds from unconscious motives is automatic and repetitive in disregard of consequences.

The study of these unconscious processes may proceed in the same way as does the investigation of any other process of personality; they are hypothetical constructs which, as parts of a theoretical system, are retained or rejected according to their success in ordering or explaining observations or in forming the basis for predictions of behavior. We proceed by observing consistent trends in behavior and on this basis conceiving of regularities of functioning in the personality; we then design experiments to test whether these hypothetical regularities of functioning express themselves in predictable ways in specified situations. The fact that a subject cannot report on his unconscious processes is only one of their manifest features; and it is a feature not easily specified, for when a subject does not report on processes we suppose are present it is difficult to tell whether he cannot, because they are unconscious, or will not, because he prefers not to reveal certain aspects of himself of which he is quite conscious. We need to bring to bear upon unconscious processes the same determined empiricism that has been directed to other aspects of personality. Meehl (1956) states that any personality variable for which criteria can be established can be measured by a scale such as the Minnesota Multiphasic Personality Inventory. A fruitful procedure, then, would be to use intensive clinical studies to delineate in more or less normal individuals such hypothetical unconscious tendencies as castration anxiety, repressed sadism, and Oedipus wishes, and on this basis to establish criteria for the development of empirical scales.

Unconscious processes in Freud's system are strictly psychological, and his followers continue to speak of these processes in the language of psychology—unconscious perception, unconscious feeling, unconscious fantasy, and so on. The old introspectionist psychology used to say "unconscious and therefore physiological." Current phenomenologists seem to take this same view of the matter, arguing that the conception of unconscious psychological processes is a contradiction in terms. Angyal (1941) urges that unconscious processes, like other hypothetical contructs in personality theory, be given a place in a formal model of personality functioning and assigned such attributes as are most helpful in predicting behavior. This general approach to the problem seems to have won considerable favor among personality theorists (Adorno and others, 1950; Frenkel-Brunswik, 1951; Klein, 1951; Murray, 1959; Rapaport, 1959; Sanford, 1966).

The status of unconscious processes of the Freudian variety in personality theory today parallels that of action theory in general. Since the late 1930s acceptance of unconscious processes as determinants of behavior has steadily increased, although they now appear to be undergoing a certain deemphasis. Psychologists who have long taken these processes for granted seem to have been showing interest in a more balanced view, as part of the current accent on the normal or the higher. Writers who have been identified with this latter trend, such as Allport (1961), Goldstein (1939), May (1959), and Rogers (1959), do not deny the validity of the Freudian dynamics so much as restrict their major role to the determination of abnormal behavior. Psychoanalytic theorists have perhaps encouraged this view by stressing for so long the crucial role of unconscious dynamics in symptom formation; but they have consistently refused to accept any categorical distinction between the normal and the abnormal, and, moreover, they have conceived of unconscious processes as motivating forces in creative and socially constructive activity. At the same time, however, they have argued that in the interests of personality integration, the unconscious should be made conscious—insofar as this is possible. Insofar as possible is a rather typical phrase in psychoanalytic writing. The point of view it expresses is strongly implicit in all tension-reduction theory. The individual does not easily reverse or even alter fundamentally his early adaptations; rather, he has to make the most of them. Differences among personality theorists respecting unconscious dynamics are mainly differences in emphasis, but variations are wide, and most writers are found at one extreme or the other. What is involved here is not a matter of arbitrary preference but contrasting views of the nature of life.

In any of the theories, when we speak of the organization of personality, we are referring eventually to the whole personality; we mean that all its parts are functionally related one to another and to the whole. Earlier in this essay, concern was expressed lest we unfairly commit certain writers to a holistic, or organismic, orientation. This caveat was perhaps overstated. As Hall and Lindzey (1957) point out, all personality theorists are holistic. Naturally they do not wish merely to breathe the word *whole* and mean thereby something that could only be spoiled by analysis. But if personality is conceived as anything more than a mere enumeration of elements, if the parts of personality are related by any operation other than mere addition, then holism is necessarily implied. Indeed, even the conception of a sum has holistic implication; the psychologist who wanted to make sure he had nothing to do with holism would have to restrict himself to enumeration or avoid the idea of personality altogether.

Of course, some psychologists do avoid the idea, studying some part function of people without considering its relations to other part functions. For example, one may concentrate on the relations of a response to external stimuli without paying any attention to the place of that response in a context of personality functioning, or one may develop a test of some performance, focusing on relations between test responses and an external criterion, without troubling about the personal meaning of those responses. But these activities have nothing to do with the psychology of personality, nor do the workers who carry them out consider themselves personality psychologists. When a student of personality engages in such research activity, he is usually careful to say that in order to obtain exact information, he is abstracting part functions from the whole to which they naturally belong.

It used to be considered virtuous when a thoroughgoing holist—Murray (1938), for example—showed a willingness to perform the analyses and to make the abstractions necessary for research. Nowadays such analysis and abstraction are taken for granted and have become second nature to the researcher in personality. All contemporary holists deny that they were ever opposed to analysis in the first place; they were only concerned that it be performed in the right way. For some time, they have been asking whether abstraction was being carried out too readily or too easily, whether investigators were forgetting to think of their variables in relation to larger wholes, and whether they were too easily satisfied with that variance in some performance which is referable to situational factors and to one or two diagnosed traits of personality.

It was stated earlier that the holistic orientation is being increasingly accepted and utilized in research design. The main point was that more contemporary theorists and researchers—such as Rogers (1951, 1959), Klein (1951), and Hilgard (1949)—are taking seriously (even insisting on) their obligations under a holistic frame of reference and finding new approaches to the study of relationships lying on what Klein has called the vertical dimension, that is, relationships between part functions and a whole, as between a characteristic of perception and the ego system or between the ego and the self.

Apparently it is very difficult to concentrate upon the inside structuring of a particular whole, such as the phenomenal self or the ego, and at the same time to give adequate attention to the transactions between this whole and the larger one in which it has a place. Thus, it is probably no accident that among those who accent the role of the ego as organizer, as a whole that influences the functioning of all its parts, many also stress the autonomy of the ego. Some writers apparently think that the ego has its own history and its own absolute strength, like a rock upon which break the waves of id impulses or of scrupulosity from the superego. This view is less holistic than that of classical psychoanalysis, which always considered that ego strength was relative to the tasks it had to perform and that statements about ego functioning had to take into account what was happening in the superego and the id. Of course, the new conception of the ego represents at least partly an effort to get away from the older and less optimistic picture of the ego as the rider of a runaway horse—a picture imputed to Freud. This picture, though no doubt somewhat unnerving, is at least as holistic as anyone could wish. It ought to be possible to construct in theoretical terms an ego that is independent of the optimism-pessimism scale, that is at least as complicated as the modern autonomous ego, and that can be seen in the context of its functional relationships with other large subsystems and the whole personality (Loevinger, 1970).

Within the whole personality, we recognize wide differences with respect to all the organizing principles touched upon in this chapter. For example, one person may be far more successful than another in getting his tendencies to respond arranged in a hierarchy or in setting up a schedule that minimizes conflicts and allows adequate gratification of a variety of needs. By paying attention to organizing activities, one may define a great many personality variables, and this, of course, has been done. Thus elements of personality as discussed in the previous chapter are by no means the only variables, for each element interacts with others and is transformed in accordance with dynamic principles. These interaction processes and equilibrating mechanisms, considered by themselves, have quantitative aspects. We may ask how frequently they are employed, how much energy is channeled through them, how much strain is required before they are called into play, how important they are relative to other processes and mechanisms, and so on. Does the individual, for example, delay gratification of one need in order to attain more gratification of this need or other needs later on, and if so, how effectively?

We can define other variables by considering certain mechanisms in relation to certain elements. Of course, as soon as we specify a few elements and define their mode of interaction with certain other specified ones, we have to deal with patterns which are complicated indeed. Yet such patterns— or syndromes, as they are sometimes called—do not altogether defy description or even certain crude forms of quantification. For example, authoritarianism (Sanford, 1956a), as a pattern of dynamic relationships among elements, takes quite similar forms in different individuals and varies in respect to quantity. It is possible to speak of the amount of an individual's authoritarianism or of the degree of his readiness to follow a latent authoritarian pattern. Much the same may be said of other patterns of personality, such as compulsiveness, narcissism, and overcompensatory dependence, that are too large and complicated to be regarded merely as traits but nonetheless have quantitative aspects.

Experimental methods have so far proved inadequate for dealing with the complexity of personality, with the vast network of meanings in which a particular pattern of behavior is likely to be entwined. Factual knowledge about the dynamic structure of personality has derived mainly from clinical work —and from the intensive study of individuals by methods originating mainly in the clinic. But psychologists, by and large, have clung to the view that propositions emerging from such "exploratory" clinical work are at best hypotheses that must be tested by laboratory methods, and they have devoted an enormous amount of energy and ingenuity to this end.

Personality research in what might be called the grand tradition was started by Murray (1938), who, more than any other psychologist, devoted himself to the task of devising methods appropriate to an organismic conception of personality. His general approach was to use a variety of tests, interviews, and projective techniques in the study of the same subjects so that particular findings on individuals could be understood in the context of a patterned organic system. The method can reveal patterns of individual functioning not previously brought to light as well as generalized part-whole relationships. The tradition is still very much alive, although the work of those who represent it constitutes today only a small part of the published investigations in the field of personality. The publication of *The Study of Lives,* edited by White (1963b) and written by eighteen psychologists who had been influenced by Murray, was an important event in the history of personality psychology.

Another approach to the study of structure is exemplified by Cattell (1959), who uses a variety of tests designed to measure variables operating on different levels of the personality and then employs correlational techniques in an effort to demonstrate dynamic relationships. Related to this approach is the effort to delineate types or syndromes of personality and on this basis to predict behavior in particular situations. Stein (1963), for example, used a self-description questionnaire to describe Peace Corps volunteers and then found that he could predict performance in the field; for example, young men who ranked high on drives for dominance and achievement and low on playfulness and sex interest, unlike all other subjects, obtained after six months in the field higher scores than before on a scale for measuring authoritarianism.

Objective and experimental studies of psychoanalytic theories have been appearing in the literature since the early

1930s. They have shown increasing sophistication both in methodology and in the derivation of testable hypotheses from Freudian theories. Examples are a study by Hall and Van de Castle (1965), who found that males reported more dreams expressive of castration anxiety while females reported more dreams expressive of castration wishes and penis envy, and a study by Zamansky (1958), who found that among hospitalized schizophrenic males, those with paranoid delusions spent more time looking at pictures of males than did those without paranoid delusions. The results of both these investigations support Freudian theories, from which the tested hypotheses were derived, but the investigators admit that their findings may, conceivably, be explained in some other way. The latter study is representative of a great many in which the effort is made to "diagnose" the subjects—often with the use of projective techniques—and on this basis to predict behavior in some controlled situation.

As we have seen, most theorists and researchers necessarily regard personality as a structure that endures at least long enough to be studied. They may speak of its organization at the time of an experimental session or during the course of a three-day assessment. Moreover, they generally agree that personality changes in lawful ways, thus exhibiting patterns. Holistic writers, such as Murray (1959) and Angyal (1941), have insisted that the life cycle of the individual is a natural unit for analysis and study. They readily agree, however, that it is very difficult to study a whole life and not inappropriate to abstract short units for intensive investigation. In practice, these short units range in length from the single experimental session to the period of childhood or that of old age.

When the psychologist speaks of a personality organization existing for a moment, he usually has in mind the psychological present, which includes all the factors necessary to predict behavior at a given time. Systematic causation of this kind is contrasted with historical causation, in which present factors are understood as traces or consequences of past events. This distinction is usually associated with Lewin. In one of his early works, Lewin (1935) made clear his intention to supply concepts and methods that would make it possible for "the experimental method to press on beyond the psychology of perception and memory to such vital problems as those with which psychoanalysis was concerned" (p. v). His efforts met with very considerable success. Numerous experimental studies (Barker, Dembo, and Lewin, 1941; Dembo, 1931; Henle, 1942, 1944; Kounin, 1941; Lewin, Dembo, Festinger, and Sears, 1944; Lewin, Lippitt, and White, 1939; Wright, 1942) show that phenomena such as regression, identification, or aggression, which have always had historical connotations in psychoanalytic literature, can be explained in terms of systematic laws. Today it is generally agreed that only present factors can explain present behavior and that traces of past events are likely to be among such factors. Investigators and practitioners still differ, however, about the importance of the past as a source of present variables and, hence, about the importance of historical inquiries as a means for finding out about presently operating consequences of past events.

The development of systematic, or ahistorical, psychology not only stimulated experimental studies of personality but also affected the practice of psychotherapy. Along with the apparent concern of the older psychoanalysis with uncovering the patient's past, psychotherapy now undertakes to change people, confining itself to the manipulation of factors operating in the present since it cannot change the past. Psychoanalysis assumes that important experiences from the past are transferred to the present and that present insight into present emotional relationships permits an individual to recall and understand his past. In psychoanalytic and psychotherapeutic practice, this view of the past as transferred to the psychological present is not necessarily related to the recent accent on the contemporary social situation or on events of the recent past as determinants of neurotic difficulties. An emphasis on systematic causation is consistent with various theories about the importance of past events or of the social situation. Thus, Ezriel (1956), while acknowledging the influence of Lewin upon his thinking, belongs mainly to the Kleinian school of psychoanalysis, according to which the events most important in the history of neuroses happen in the first year of life. Nonetheless he urges that in the psychoanalysis of individuals and groups, all interpretations should be transference interpretations, directed to events of the here and now.

To find the past in the present is not the only task of the researcher or psychotherapist who wishes to understand personality in accordance with systematic laws. He must also find something of the future in the present. If personality is, as Murray and Kluckhohn (1948) say, "an ongoing manifold of structured processes," then some, perhaps many, of the processes that we may observe right now have functional roles in the promotion of long-range objectives, which must be appreciated in order for us to understand the processes. Obviously one cannot always tell where a person is going just by noting the direction in which he is headed; one may have to follow him a way in order to form a reasonable hypothesis (to say nothing of whether he reaches his intended or apparent destination). Similarly, as Chein (1947) points out, finding the past in the present requires not only detecting traces of remote events but also noting "unfinished business"—unresolved conflicts or unfulfilled needs which were initiated days or weeks or years ago but which still organize many of the present observable processes.

Considerations of this kind primarily have led personality theorists to say that one can study short periods of personal life only by abstracting a part from the whole. Even while agreeing that we cannot tell all about a process without seeing it in the context of larger temporal wholes, researchers on personality can nevertheless tell something, and they have proceeded to do the best they can.

But another issue is involved here. How is the concept of systematic causation affected by the length of time we observe our subjects? If we see the present as organized partly by long-range objectives and if we predict the future from the present on this basis, we have only systematic principles to guide us. And, presumably, the unfinished business that organizes present processes persists in accordance with the same dynamic laws that hold for strivings in general, allowing one to investigate a temporal unit of behavior that lasts a week or longer and still to stay within the framework of systematic causation. Certain variables that were operating at the start are measured, and the final state of affairs is predicted according to some dynamic hypothesis. For example, one may predict that a humiliating experience experimentally induced will be recalled better after a week or a month than after an hour and may make tests at the stated times. But the same period can be studied with attention to historical causation, by surveying the major events of the period and noting which had left traces at the end, or taking a sample of the subject's verbal responses— some dreams or a word-association test—and noting which ones can be traced to the events of the preceding week or months. In fact, an investigator working on remembered humiliation would be likely to supplement his systematic study with a historical one, thus exploring the possibility that a knowledge of intervening events might help explain some of the exceptions to his rule.

If one can make an investigation of systematic causation over a month, he can do the same for a longer period, using the same general procedure. Naturally, as the time span increases, the intervention of factors not taken into account at the beginning is very likely to increase also, making the task of controlling these factors very difficult. Either one may concentrate on one or a very few cases and try to keep a record of all important happenings, or one may use many subjects, hoping to cancel out enough of the accidental factors. In work of this kind, a concern with historical factors is regarded as a concern with individual differences. The early experimental work of Lewin and his associates concerned the pure case or the general law. As in much present animal experimentation, they could throw out cases that varied so greatly from the group in some particular that they did not fulfill the conditions of the experiment. Nowadays the researcher in personality often combines systematic and historical modes of investigation, with a probable trend toward increasing use of the historical method, in an effort to identify and measure more of the factors operating in the present and thus to discover laws of greater generality.

This approach ordinarily involves fairly large blocks of time. To observe the consistency in behavior from which we infer factors of personality, the subject must be seen in varied situations—a time-consuming process. Once subjects are "known" through clinical studies or surveys of their characteristic responses, they may be placed in laboratory situations for intensive investigation of particular processes. One may either control the personality factors while concentrating on the effects of a particular situation (for example, Christie, 1952; Cowen, Landes, and Schaet, 1959; Eager and Smith, 1952; Steiner, 1968) or direct attention to the role of personality factors in the determination of some particular kind of behavior (for example, Block and Block, 1951; Fisher, 1951; Hollander, 1953; Rokeach, 1948; Alfert, 1967). This approach seems to be preferred by personality psychologists today; it stands in contrast both to Lewin's earlier approach, which tended to ignore individual differences, and to the more traditional approach of experimental psychology, which sought to rule out individual differences by the use of many subjects.

With increased understanding of systematic and historical causation and the relations between them, some psychologists are more willing than before to use experimental methods to study processes that take time, as in research on the effects of psychotherapy (for example, Coch and French, 1948; Katz and Stotland, 1959; Newcomb, 1958; Sarnoff and Katz, 1954) and on the relation of present personality organization to future performance (for example, Fishman, 1960; Holt and Luborsky, 1958; Kelly and Fiske, 1951). Whereas such studies may cover time spans as long as the four years of college, for example, they are still systematic as long as they focus upon the effects of factors determined at the beginning.

Impressed by the durability of these factors, personality

psychologists of the action frame of reference have favored the historical approach. They have been most concerned with tendencies in the person which persist through time and enter into the determination of behavior in diverse situations. Lewin and his early associates could neglect historical causation because they considered that the apparent persistence of tendencies was due to the persistence of field conditions. In practice, as we have seen, they often defined field conditions mainly as what was going on in the objective environment. If personality depended on field conditions and changed as they changed, obviously there was little point in making case studies to discover what differences in readiness to respond the individuals brought to the experimental situation.

Although all theorists conceive of a more or less stable structure, some accent the more and some the less; some are inclined to stress the apparent fixity of inner structures and the continuity of the past and the present, while others stress change with circumstances and the possibility of new beginnings. In the history of thought, these contrasting views of man have taken many forms. Perhaps the contrast has been sharpest in the philosophies of Nazism and Marxism, the former holding that an individual is totally determined once and for all by his blood or race, the latter that personality is merely a reflection of the social-economic system in which the individual lives. In common sense and in folklore the two views seem to have competed on more or less even terms.

The theories of psychoanalysis (Freud, 1938, 1959; Klein, 1948; Rapaport, 1959), with their heavy emphasis upon childhood traumata and repression, have stressed persistence. So have stimulus-response theories. Although they also attempt to explain change, their accent on the continuity of the past and the present justifies their classification with theories that stress the importance of early events in the determination of personality and later behavior (Dollard and Miller, 1950; Sears, 1951b). Both psychoanalysis and behaviorism, as we have seen, are heavily environmentalistic in stressing experience rather than genetic factors to account for individual differences in personality. In contrast with situationism (Sherif, 1936), field theory (Lewin, 1935), and certain cognitive theories (for example, Asch, 1952) which generally accent the possibilities of change through responsiveness to changing situations or through cognitive abilities that have been developed, psychoanalysis and behaviorism stress the environment of the past rather than of the present and the persistence of structures into the present.

However, few psychologists today seem disposed to state the issue in such general terms or to take a position on one side or the other. All theorists recognize the necessity for dealing with both persistence and change, with attention to different structures, different conditions, and different kinds and mechanisms of change (Cattell and Cross, 1952; Katz and Stotland, 1959; Kelman and Cohler, 1959; Sarnoff and Katz, 1954). Theorists differ, however, in how they account for change. Those who put little structure into the personality have little difficulty; personality changes as the social situation or the social field conditions change. For that matter, these theorists have a ready explanation of persistence too, for the social and cultural structures that are supposed to determine the organization of personality are often very durable.

Theorists who concentrate on the building up of structures during the early years are not inclined to suppose that these structures will yield to change without a struggle. According to psychoanalytic theory and probably to action theory in general, the most durable structures of the personality do not change essentially unless their unconscious sources are made conscious to the subject. Stimulus-response psychologists, of course, attempt to bring change as well as persistence under the same set of general principles; thus, for example, a response does not persist unless it is reinforced, but the possible reinforcing agencies in the person become in time very numerous and very complicated. The theorists of this group—those who accent determination in the early years of life—do not deny that personality can and does change as a result of interactions with the environment, but they insist that these changes are consistent with the individual's past and with his presently operating tendencies. In general, these theorists proceed in accordance with the tension-reduction principle: the personality system (or any subsystem of it) changes when it encounters strain of such quality and intensity that old adaptive responses do not suffice, and new ones have to be improvised; and within the responses possible in a given developmental status, the system handles the strain in the way that involves the least general disturbance to itself.

Writers who do not restrict themselves to the principle of homeostasis sometimes accent the individual's potential for change and sometimes his capacity for self-consistency despite radically changing circumstances. These writers (for example, G. W. Allport, 1955; Maslow, 1954; Jahoda, 1958) are concerned less with the persistence-change dimension than with the higher versus the lower. If a situational determinist presents his views, these writers reply by calling attention to the individual's capacity to maintain a stable self-conception, to act in accordance with a consistent system of values, and to carry out long-term programs of rational action. If, on the other hand, an individual presents an unfortunate pattern of behavior that has endured for years and thus is presumably based on personality structures, these writers are likely to consider with hope the prospects of change after a few hours of therapy devoted to bringing about cognitive restructuring or changes in the conception of the self. (Such a case may lead a psychoanalyst to think of a two-year course of treatment and a behaviorist of a rigorous program of deconditioning.) The fact that changes do occur in such therapy has led these writers to conclude that the psychoanalytic and behaviorist theories of determination must be wrong. Representatives of these latter views reply, of course, that the changes under consideration are superficial or temporary.

These contrasting views are not so much in conflict as they often appear to be. Sometimes different writers are talking about different kinds of structures in the personality. Not only are there different mechanisms of change and different determinants of consistency, but some are more applicable than others to certain personality structures. We have seen that among ways of classifying the structures of personality, several are theoretically more or less neutral—the outer and the inner, the central and the peripheral, the phenotypic and the genotypic, the conscious and the unconscious. Could we not likewise observe that subsystems of any of these groupings may be momentary, temporary, or enduring? If so, then different hypotheses are required to explain the different states of the different subsystems.

Studies of stability and change in personality structures have not been widespread in recent years, owing chiefly to the expense and inherent difficulty of testing the same individuals at several points in their lives. Longitudinal studies aroused much interest in the 1920s and 1930s, when several major ones were begun (Cox, 1926; Jones, 1938; Jones and Bayley, 1941; Macfarlane, 1960); they were rather neglected in favor of experimental and assessment studies during the 1940s and 1950s but are now staging something of a comeback (Carlson, 1965; Emmerick, 1968; Mann and Janis, 1968; Zigler, Balla, and Butterfield, 1968). Nevertheless, if we take the whole period from 1926 to the present, the accumulation of such studies has been very considerable. As an example of what can be learned from them, we may consider the work of Kagan and Moss (1962). These investigators focused on a group of young people who grew to maturity between 1929 and 1958, finding that many patterns of behavior exhibited by children during the years three to ten predicted theoretically related patterns of behavior in early adulthood, such as involvement in intellectual mastery, sex role identification, and spontaneity. From a review of several hundred longitudinal studies, Bloom (1964) concluded that the experiences of early childhood have great implications for all that follows in the individual's life and that although personality may change at any age under the impact of a sufficiently powerful environment, change in many characteristics becomes increasingly difficult with increasing age. He believes, however, that environmental conditions favor-

able to the child's development will be identified, and made
to exist, in this century.

In summary, we see that personality is usually conceived
of as a more or less stable structure that endures long enough
for studies to be made. It exists always as a subsystem in larger
social systems, but it is possible to concentrate for the moment
upon its inside structuring. The term *structure* refers here to
all the relationships within personality, including the formal
ones. One way to describe order or pattern in personality is to
use a spatial model in which parts are arranged in relation to
each other and to the whole. Such analysis may prepare the
way for explanation in dynamic terms, that is to say, in terms
of lawful transformations of parts and transactions among parts.

According to the prevailing action frame of reference,
the major organizing principle is that of striving to reduce tension or to restore equilibrium. Diverse resources are mobilized
and organized as equilibrating mechanisms. This general formula holds for any subsystem of the personality that has been
the object of tension-producing stimulation. But personality,
in the minds of most theorists, consists of very numerous subsystems, of which many are subjected to some strain at the
same time—hence the necessity for organization on a larger
scale, for such acts as coordination, scheduling, or establishing
hierarchies.

The tension-reduction formula has been the object of
much criticism. One line of criticism has led to general agreement that the states of equilibrium existing before and after
striving are not usually the same since individuals change in
the course of their strivings. Another line of criticism is simply
that the tension-reduction formula is not enough to account
for all the activities of the organism; there is also tension generation, self-expression, and the triggering of affects by a variety
of stimuli. This line of criticism has been sufficiently effective
so that psychologists are now energetically seeking a more general theory of human motivation.

In considering the sources of organizing tendencies in
behavior and personality, some theorists accent the original

nature of man; others, what is developed during the individual's life; and still others, the regularities in the contemporary social and cultural environment. The view that personality is from the beginning more organized and able to organize than behaviorism or psychoanalysis have traditionally supposed has been gaining ground. Some writers accent natural growth trends and the autonomous ego, others stick to the tension-reduction formula. The issue may be illuminated to some extent by viewing it in a social-historical context, but it remains basically an empirical one.

Situationism, certain tendencies in field theory, and modern theories of interpersonal relations have minimized organization in the individual personality and have accented the social group and the culture as the organizers of human behavior and human life. In the face of arguments from these schools of thought, the student of personality has usually stood his ground, reiterating his preference for studying the individual human, whose organized dispositions structure the situations he encounters. Nevertheless, as in the case of elements, personality theory has gradually become more social, with more concern for the articulation of personality systems and social systems, for how the more or less autonomous structures of the personality are sustained by surrounding social forces.

The literature on personality often differentiates processes that are conscious, processes that are not but are capable of becoming so, and processes that are forcibly prevented from becoming so. Activities directed to the management of a new stimulus or problem are considered most likely to be conscious, while habitual responses or devices for automatic adjustment are not. The unconscious, in the Freudian sense, refers to processes that have been rendered unconscious, usually in childhood, because this procedure was the only available means for adapting to severe strains. Adaptations of this kind are not easily reversed; they tend to persist, to function in accordance with their own special dynamics, to enter into diverse functional relationships with other structures of the personality. The Freudian view of the unconscious has gradually won wide acceptance among psychologists, particularly since the mid 1930s, but it is undergoing a certain deemphasis at the present time—an aspect of the current preoccupation with the normal and the higher.

When psychologists speak of the organization of personality, they are almost always referring to the whole personality. All personality psychologists are holistic in the sense of believing that all particular response characteristics have functional roles in the operations of the whole. In practice, however, they often abstract part functions from their natural place in the whole to study them more closely—a procedure now so routine that one wonders whether many personality psychologists have not forgotten their true holistic position. However we are now witnessing a fresh impulse to take holism seriously and to deliberately design researches to reveal the significance of part functions in larger totalities. This trend is best exemplified by work on the ego and the self. One may hope that concentration on the inside structuring of these large elements of personality may be sustained even while their dependence upon the functioning of the whole that includes them is given the attention it deserves.

Like the elements of personality discussed earlier, interaction processes and equilibrating mechanisms have quantitative aspects, may be treated as variables of personality, and when considered with the particular elements they affect, yield patterns or syndromes of personality which also have quantitative aspects.

FOUR

≈≈≈≈≈≈≈≈≈≈≈≈≈≈≈≈≈≈≈≈≈≈≈≈≈≈≈≈

Boundaries
of Personality

≈≈≈≈≈≈≈≈≈≈≈≈≈≈≈≈≈≈≈≈≈≈≈≈≈≈≈≈≈≈

A complete definition of personality must deal not only with elements and their organization but with the problem of distinguishing personality from phenomena closely related to it. We have already mentioned the view that personality is to be distinguished from overt behavior and from the environment with which it interacts. According to various theorists, personality should also be distinguished from the effect of the individual's behavior upon his environment, social or other, and from the physical structure and physiological processes of the individual. However, each of these orders of phenomena is included in one or more of the definitions presented at the beginning of this essay. The whole problem of boundaries is difficult and controversial, and at present one's position with respect to this problem is bound to involve some commitment to a particular theoretical approach and, probably, a degree of arbitrariness.

Allport (1937b) stated as explicitly as anyone that personality is not the same thing as behavior or activity. "It is what lies behind specific acts and within the individual" (p. 218). "The systems that constitute personality are in every sense determining tendencies and, when aroused by suitable stimuli, provoke those adjustive and expressive acts by which the personality comes to be known" (p. 49). White (1955) gives a contemporary expression of the same point of view: "To say that we measure the achievement motive is metaphorical, not literal. Our measures give us but hints of what lies hidden in the person being tested. . . . The index has something to do with achievement motivation" (p. 97).

In the 1937 statement just quoted, Allport was opposing a trend then current in behavioristic theory, an attempt to contrive a psychology without an organism by limiting the field's attention to objectively observable stimuli and objectively observable responses. Insofar as personality existed for writers who expressed this view, it had to consist of behavior, of observable stimulus-response relationships. Undoubtedly all personality theorists preferring the action frame of reference agree with Allport's critique.

Unlike its early version, modern stimulus-response theory does not presume to get along without any hypothetical constructs at all, at least when it is directed to the phenomena of personality. Indeed, the "stimulus" itself is often necessarily hypothetical (Guthrie, 1952). When it is assumed that all responses are instigated by stimuli, the problem is often to find the stimuli that are provoking observed responses. While the investigator is conducting his quest for a stimulus, it exists, we may suppose, in his mind's eye. Similarly, habit, which in stimulus-response theory stands for any stable or enduring characteristic of a person, appears to be a hypothetical construct. Not all the habits that an individual has learned, which together are said to make up his personality, can possibly be observed at any one time, yet they exist somewhere in the structure of the person. They may be theoretically observable when our techniques of observation become sufficiently advanced. In the meanwhile, there is at least some gap between what is observed and what is conceived to exist—presumably in the functioning of the individual's nervous system.

The most characteristic feature of modern stimulus-response theory is not that it dispenses with hypothetical constructs altogether but that it strives to use no more of such concepts than is absolutely necessary and to maintain the closest possible ties between what is conceived and what is observed. Modern stimulus-response theory is reflected in the definitions of personality by McClelland (1951) and Hilgard (1953) quoted near the start of this essay. These definitions, more than any of the others quoted, strive to keep behavior—rather than systems, processes, or dispositions—in the center of attention. For McClelland, personality is the "conceptualization of a person's behavior," not a description of it. For Hilgard, personality is "the sum total of individual characteristics and ways of behaving which in their organization or patterning describe an individual's unique adjustment to his environment." While Allport speaks of personality as "determining the individual's unique adjustments," Hilgard says "describe." This distinction is another example of the stimulus-response theorist's tendency to be cautious and objective and to ascribe no more to the "insides" of the person than is necessary. In the passage quoted earlier in this chapter, White (1955) suggests that this tendency sometimes leads the stimulus-response psychologist into serious error. So eager is he to keep concepts and observables closely tied together that he sometimes mistakes one for the other. Even when far from claiming that personality is embraced by overt behavior, he nonetheless tends to act as if this were so because, as it seems, overt behavior is relatively easy to get hold of.

The idea of relatively loose (or remote and complicated)

relationships between measures of overt behavior and what lies hidden in the person being tested—the absence of a one-to-one correlation in any population of subjects—is surely one of the most cherished ideas in the dynamic theorist's scheme of things. The same (or very similar) measured behavior may be ascribed to different processes in the personality in different individuals or in the same individual at different times. And conversely, the same personality process may express itself in different observable ways. The beauty of a concept like achievement motive is not that a simple operation in a laboratory can measure it but that it helps explain a consistent trend of behavior in a variety of situations—the congruence, one may say, of a variety of measures. And together with other concepts, the achievement motive can help explain the more complex phenomena of everyday behavior. One must proceed, of course, by measuring what can be measured and by demonstrating relationships among measures. But personality processes themselves are not measured; they are invoked to explain observed relationships and to predict relationships that will be observed under specified conditions. So long as the concepts are tied to observations, this use of personality concepts and theory, as we have seen, is no departure from operationism. And without this use, how would the personality theorist maintain his freedom to think about his material?

In an essential way, then, the distinction between personality and behavior is the distinction between the concept and that which is observable. But one may ask how the matter should be handled if it turns out that what was once conceived can now be observed directly—if, for example, someone should contrive an instrument from which we would read directly variations that until now we had imagined occurring in some component of personality. There are two answers to this question. One is that the possibilities of ever finding such perfect indexes of personality variables are remote—and seem to be becoming more so. When Tolman (1936, 1938) and later Hull (1943) and their numerous followers worked with intervening variables in the 1930s, the hope and expectation was

that means of linking inferred explanatory concepts unequivo-
cally to observables would be found. As Koch (1959) points
out, this quest has been virtually abandoned. Not only did
Tolman (1936, 1938) change his mind about the possibility of
measuring intervening variables by defining experiments, but
many psychologists now agree with Lazarsfeld's (1959) argument
that for any intervening variable, a variety of indicators cor-
respond. Lazarsfeld believes his argument applies even to animal experimentation. When we come to the human personality,
the discovery of specific indicators of theoretical variables is
virtually out of the question.

The other answer to the question about the direct reading of personality is based on simple logic. If personality is
defined as something that, among other things, helps to determine observed behavior, then it cannot at the same time be
observed behavior. If one can observe it, then it is not personality. Of course, we may someday be able to observe
phenomena that have been generated solely by personality
processes, conceivably by getting at the brain directly. But
these phenomena would certainly not be behavior in the usual
sense of responses or acts of people.

The question of the impact upon personality of changes
in behavior has been the subject of much discussion, owing
largely to an extraordinary revival of interest in using conditioned response techniques to alter undesirable patterns of
behavior. In 1958, in *Psychotherapy by Reciprocal Inhibition,*
Wolpe described the apparently successful application to adult
neurotic patients of techniques used in the 1920s by Watson
and Jones in overcoming children's specific fears. (For example,
a child's fear of an animal could be overcome by repeatedly
associating the animal with pleasant experiences.) Wolpe's
cause was soon taken up by Eysenck (1959), a persistent and
somewhat free-swinging critic of psychoanalysis, who labeled
Wolpe's procedure behavior therapy and, with some disregard
for the usual cautions in evaluating research on psychotherapy,
made rather extravagant claims for the "new" therapy. Since
then there has been a great deal of activity on this front

(Mattarazzo, 1965; Fisher and Harris, 1966). Various procedures for extinguishing maladaptive responses and for rewarding desirable ones have been developed, so that there has now appeared what may almost be called a school of psychotherapy. Its proponents claim that these procedures remove symptoms more effectively than any other method of treatment, that return of symptoms is rare, and that symptoms are not supplanted by others.

Eysenck considers behavior therapy a direct challenge to psychoanalysis, both to its practice and to its theory. It is, indeed, a challenge to all psychotherapists who assume that a person's problems have something to do with his subjective experience and that he ought somehow to participate as a conscious being in what happens to him in the therapeutic encounter. Psychotherapists of this turn of mind are extremely skeptical of the claims for behavior therapy. They admit that almost any behavior can be changed by sufficiently powerful, or shrewdly programed, stimuli, but they doubt that such proceedings have no ill effects upon the person and that symptoms do not return in some other guise. For example, after discovering that a woman's phobia of going down steps was based on her feeling that to do so meant going out into the street and becoming a streetwalker, a psychoanalyst would probably admit that by heroic conditioning she could be induced to walk down stairs, but he would not therefore lose interest in how she managed her unrecognized wish to become a prostitute. He would be extremely skeptical of follow-up studies of therapeutic efficacy done by psychologists who did not believe in unconscious wishes or in the possibility of a connection between a phobia and a desire to become a streetwalker. Should he expect behavior therapists to hunt very diligently for other problematic manifestations in people whose behavior had been changed by conditioning? Moreover, since stimulus-response psychologists use so few concepts to stand for processes in the inner life of the person, they might be slow to recognize such changes as had occurred.

Critics of behavior therapy also raise questions concerning the causes of the reported changes in symptoms. One of the oldest and most widely accepted propositions in the whole literature on psychotherapy is that in the hands of a warm-hearted and enthusiastic practitioner who has faith in his method, almost any therapeutic procedure can bring reduction in symptoms. Stimulus-response therapists, typically, have focused on the conditioning program itself, paying little attention to variables that enter into the relationship between a therapist and his patient.

Fundamental to this whole argument is the division, discussed above, between stimulus-response psychologists and dynamic-organismic theorists. The former consider that a stimulus makes its way into an organism without disturbing anything in the areas about its course, finds its target, and thus sends an expected response on its solitary way to the surface. Dynamic-organismic theorists, on the other hand, think of a stimulus as initiating changes, however slight, throughout the whole system, evoking numerous "responses," most of them only remotely related to the original stimulus. From the point of view of dynamic-organismic theory, behavior therapy should be classed with a group of procedures (including hypnosis, Alcoholics Anonymous, and various kinds of drug therapy) which induce changes in particular patterns of behavior without the affected person's knowing what is happening to him, without any expansion of consciousness or of the individual's capacity for further development. Dynamic-organismic theorists may reject behavior therapy for the same reasons that Freud gave up hypnosis: Patients did not incorporate material uncovered by hypnosis (behavior changes) into their conscious selves, and Freud did not like to have the kind of power over people that hypnosis gave him.

What the dynamic-organismic theorist can learn from the therapeutic activities of stimulus-response psychologists is that people who are very ill psychologically are still responsive to the environment of the moment—not only to programs for extinguishing particular maladaptive responses but also to programs for expanding the response repertory and for bringing

into awareness areas of the environment previously meaningless. This lesson is an important antidote to those over-
simplified versions of Freudian theory in which everything of
consequence in the personality is still tied to processes in the
sphere of conflict and can be modified only by making the
unconscious conscious. A change in behavior, induced by conditioning, may indeed lead to a change in personality; it may,
for example, lead to changes in the way a person is perceived
by others, and these changes may lead to a change in the way
he perceives himself, which may lead to a more significant
change in behavior—and so on. In short, a single change in
behavior induced by bringing fresh stimuli to bear may set in
motion a process of change that may in time have implications
for large areas of the personality. Stimulus-response psychologists could make fuller use of their own studies if they were
to look beyond their working assumption that the processes
affected by particular stimuli are separate. We have good reason to believe that different structures of the person (for example, unconscious as contrasted with conscious) change under
different conditions and through the operation of different
mechanisms. Stimulus-response psychologists could contribute
in an important way to our understanding of these matters,
especially if they were to develop some curiosity about, and
use some imagination in conceiving of, the structures to be
changed.

The effect of a person's behavior upon others, his social
stimulus value, is often very impressive. In the past, some
writers were so struck by these effects that they regarded them
as the chief data or even as the defining substance of personality. If, however, we are to separate personality and behavior,
we must separate personality and the effects of behavior by the
same logic. The typical effects of a person's behavior—not only
his influence upon other people, but his creations, constructions, and achievements—are expressive of his personality and
important sources of inferences about it. But such effects as
we are able to observe usually have other determinants besides

personality, and there is more to personality than can ever be perceived in its effects.

Although personality and the effects of personality in action are different, they may nevertheless be seen as parts of a person-environment system. In this view, the individual and his social environment constitute a dynamic configuration whose parts are so closely related that drawing lines of demarcation is often very difficult. Some theorists prefer to make this configuration (rather than personality itself) the unit for study; others emphasize factors in the field surrounding the individual so much that the concept of personality barely retains its integrity. For example, Sullivan (1953) stresses the interpersonal relationship, and Sears (1951a) the dyad. This preference is largely due to the rapid development of social science during the past three or four decades, but it may also owe something to the declining parochialism of American scientists; Murphy (1958) states that Western thought overstresses the separation of man from his social context. My view is that in a universe of related events it is necessary to be arbitrary to some extent and that we do well to study one order of events without studying all the other orders to which it is related. Thus we may separate personality and the environment conceptually and study any interesting relations between them.

But how are the boundary lines to be drawn? One's approach to this problem depends on the conceptual model of personality functioning one adopts. Common sense suggests that a man's personality is somewhere inside him, under his skin, and that as his body carries this structure into different environments, it somehow remains much the same or at least maintains some consistency within itself. According to this view, personality must be located in nature. Sophisticated versions take into account what we know about bodily functioning and without hesitation place the seat of personality in the brain, the conserver of experience and the integrator of processes. Personality is thus postafferent and preefferent. From this point of view, the task of distinguishing between personality and the environment is no different from that of distinguishing between, for example, a memory image and the physical stimulus that gave rise to it. Processes involving a change in the form of energy intervene between the two. Not all the processes of personality that we may infer from the observation of behavior have any known correlates in brain functioning as yet. Supposing, as we must, that such correlates may ultimately be discovered, we are free to conceptualize brain processes to explain our observations, taking care that we do not contradict what is known about brain functioning. This would be using a physiological model of personality processes.

The other main model of personality is the formal model. A circle (or an ellipse or some such figure) represents the personality, which is surrounded by an area known as the environment. What separates personality from the environment is the boundary, to which the theorist attempts to ascribe whatever properties order the phenomena, accord with known facts, and promise to aid in the discovery of new ones. In this way Lewin (1935) distinguished between the person and the psychological environment, and between the life space—which embraced both the person and his psychological environment —and the nonpsychological (or geographical) environment. He endowed boundaries between these regions with the property of permeability, and he conceived of them in dynamic terms as offering resistance to exchange of energy between neighboring systems. Miller (1955), in presenting what he calls "general behavior systems theory, a subcategory of general systems theory," pointed out that the boundaries of systems (such as those of personality) are not always clear cut, that a given individual or behaving subsystem may be a part of several systems, and that the essential fact about a boundary is that any exchange of energy across it leads to some change in the energy form.

Proceeding in this general way, we may conceptualize as many systems and subsystems as we like and define their boundaries in theoretical terms. But finding empirical support for these conceptualizations or showing that one of them fits the facts better than some other are different matters. It is sometimes very difficult to say whether a given variable is in the personality or the environment. Perhaps, as Miller suggests, it is in both. Certainly we may observe personality-environment relationships that seem just as bounded as does the personality itself. However, we are not without guides to the location of variables. According to a purely formal criterion, for example, a variable is in the personality system if the operations of that variable can be deduced from personality processes. Or we may view the matter in probabilistic terms: A unit may be said to be incorporated by personality insofar as the variance due to personality is greater than the variance due to the environment. Or making use of a homeostatic model, we may consider that personality imposes limits on the range of variation in behavior that can be elicited by the environment.

The great benefit of formal models is that they suggest what to look for—in particular, they direct our attention to areas that may otherwise be neglected. In this respect, Lewin's conception of the psychological environment has been a contribution of great importance. In the early thirties, when Lewin's views were just beginning to have an impact in this country, American psychologists (except where psychoanalysis was influential) were seriously neglecting the organism in their attempt to construct an objective stimulus-response psychology. The conception of psychological environment called proper attention to the world in which the individual lives, the world of his experience, his hopes and aspirations, his fears. Psychoanalysis with its inner world, Murray (1938) with his concept of beta press (the stimulus situation as perceived by the subject), Murphy (1947) with his biosocial theory, and Rogers (1951) with his phenomenology, all soon ensured the psychological environment of an adequate role in personality theory. Today, the psychological environment or some very similar conception has a very important place in the thinking of most personality theorists, and research is flourishing on relationships involving the individual's cognitions, interpretations, constructions, and the like. Indeed, Lewin and Rogers, like the psychoanalysts before them, have been accused of paying far too little attention to the world of reality—a criticism which perhaps also affects the reception of Kelly's work (1953).

From the point of view of common sense and the physiological model, the psychological environment is inside the personality; individuals respond to a feeling of being rejected or to a sense of lowered self-esteem. Clearly, however, these phenomena are postafferent and must be correlated with events in the physical (or what Lewin called the geographical) environment—either that of the present or that of the past. Theorists may differ in the importance they attach to this environment, but none can justify its complete neglect. Happily, there is no reason in theory why a psychologist cannot be interested in both the geographical and the psychological environments, in their interrelationships, and in the relations of each or both in the functioning of the person. But he must recognize that in order to study relationships involving the geographical, or "real," environment, he must specify its stimuli without benefit of a subject's perception of it. This is no easy matter, particularly in the case of the all-important social environment. One can learn a great deal about an individual's psychological environment by the relatively comfortable procedure of listening to him talk about himself or by the highly respectable procedure of placing him in a number of carefully controlled experimental situations. But to characterize the "real" environment in which he lives from day to day requires special methods and techniques—and a great deal of legwork. In clinical practice, for example, psychotherapy is the preferred method for understanding and treating the disturbed individual, although where time is limited and action is called for, therapists can suggest no substitute for visits to the patient's home or interviews with members of his family (and possibly with other relevant people) by a trained social worker. Again, in the earliest attempts at personality assessment, psychologists sought to predict the individual's future behavior on the basis of intensive studies removed from his ordinary social environment. This procedure persisted long after it was generally recognized that tests and interviews with the individual ought to be supplemented by visits to his home, interviews with his spouse, observations of him on the job, and studies of other institutions within which he performs in social roles; the difficulties and expense of such investigation seemed too great. But more recent assessment studies, such as the assessment of prospective ministers by Stern, Stein, and Bloom (1956), have tried to formulate the demands of the subject's situation and to obtain measures of them—the requirements of his roles and the values and practices of the institution in which he works, for example. Other examples of special studies of the environment are the work of Pace and Stern (1958) in devising a special instrument for studying the characteristics of colleges; the work of Freedman (1956), Sanford (1958a), Thistlethwait (1959), Brown (1962), Katz and others (1968), and Constantinople (1969) in predicting students' performances and in specifying features of the institutional setting relevant to personality development; the complete survey, summary, and evaluation of this work by Feldman and Newcomb (1969); the well-known ecological studies of Barker and Wright (1949, 1955); and the investigations by Bott (1957) of the individual in his family and social network. Such studies are concerned with improving the prediction of behavior by taking into account a range of factors in the personality and in the social environment. They do not meet our need for understanding how the social system operates within the individual at any given time and how the individual may have an impact upon the social system, or systems, within which he lives.

The process of interaction is clarified by Erikson's (1950) concept of ego identity. When a person has ego identity, in Erikson's meaning of the term, his sense of identity is confirmed to some degree by the perceptions and treatments of him by other people, congruent with and based partly upon the role structure that exists in society. Thus a radical change in these aspects of the social system would change the ego identity. Bettelheim's (1943) observations in a concentration

camp showed some of the ways in which the ego was broken
down, and some of the ways in which it was preserved, under
the Nazi program for enslavement. In my observations on the
imposition of a loyalty oath at a university (Sanford, 1966) I
showed how the individual superego was altered as a result
of a social crisis. These studies strongly suggest that extreme
social change may radically alter even relatively stable structures of the personality, whether or not these deeply based
structures are sustained by previous social stability.

If changes in a social structure change the people who
occupy its roles, then we should expect it to be at least as difficult to change such a structure by deliberate plan as to change
an individual. This indeed seems to be the case, as any social
scientist who has tried to bring about some mild reform in his
university or department can testify. People vest interest in
their organizational roles, using them not only for rational
ends but for defensive purposes and for the gratification of
unconscious needs; and thus when changes in organizations are
instituted from above, much seemingly irrational protest is
heard. Anyone who would change the role structure of an
organization (by manipulating the incentives for desired role
performances, for example) has to be guided by a theory of the
interactions among the complex structures of the person and
not by just a few simple assumptions about universal human
needs. The same consideration holds for social actions affecting masses of people, actions that now so often fail in their
purpose and are followed by various unanticipated consequences. Social analysis can be aided by an assessment of what
Fromm (1941) calls social character, a socially shaped structure
embodying deep emotional needs and common to most members of the group in question. For example, if the social character of Group A is authoritarian, we should not expect that
its prejudices against Group B would be ameliorated very
much by an exchange program.

The reasons for studying the organism as a whole, for
regarding all the biological and psychological processes that
take place under a person's skin as parts of a single system, are

at least as cogent as the reasons for regarding the individual and his environment as a system. The question is whether we should equate personality with the organism as a whole as some writers have done (for example, Eysenck, 1953) or should regard personality as a separate system that interacts with other systems of the organism. The matter is particularly complicated if we regard personality as an organization of processes in the brain and thus make no categorical distinction between personality functioning and other biological events. Yet it would be inconsistent with this essay not to prefer to distinguish personality from the constitution and to study the relations between the two. Indeed, this practice seems to be the most common one among personality theorists.

In research in this field, sometimes the bodily process and sometimes the personality function is the independent variable. The former proceeding is illustrated by studies of the effects on personality of damage to the brain (Goldstein, 1959) or by studies in which gross variations in bodily form or function are considered to be perceived by an individual who responds in accordance with his needs and values—as in the case of a physical handicap, for example (Landis and Bolles, 1942). Research in which the personality process is treated as the independent variable is illustrated by studies which indicate that prolonged psychological disturbances lead to changes in organ systems—ulcers of the stomach, for example (Mittelman, Wolff, and Schorf, 1942). However, research is commonly directed to producing correlations between physical and physiological variables on the one hand and personality variables on the other—explanation then being sought in terms of complex interactions between the two sets of variables. This is true, for example, of studies stimulated by Sheldon's (1940, 1954) classic and influential work on physique and personality. Sheldon, of course, emphasizes the biological basis of his somatotypes and offers hypotheses to explain how the individual's bodily constitution helps to determine some of his characteristic behavior. Sheldon admits, however, that the somatotypes may change under the impact of nutritional or other environmental

changes, and other psychologists (Hall and Lindzey, 1957; Sanford, 1956c) have been ready with hypotheses to explain how
personality processes may influence physique.

Although literature on the relations between bodily
processes and psychological factors is vast (Barker, Wright,
and Gonick, 1946; Dunbar, 1938; Shock, 1944; Sanford and
others, 1943), this whole area has been rather neglected by
personality psychologists. This neglect may be attributed to our
American cultural history—we are optimistic environmental-
ists. It may also be attributed to the way the scientific disciplines are organized—psychosomatic relationships have been
more or less claimed by the medical profession. Unquestionably, the varied and complicated relationships between personality and bodily processes constitute a rich and relatively
unexplored field for investigation. Personality psychologists in
general continue to neglect this field, but they seem to regard
the investigation of bodily processes as at least important
enough to suggest that physiological psychologists ought to
study not only the central nervous system but those other
bodily processes in which personality seems to have a determining role. They will probably have to do it themselves, for
the physiological psychologist typically is after bigger game—
the processes underlying the functioning of personality itself.

Among other concepts traditionally related to personality, character and temperament seem to have virtually dis-
appeared from the literature as technical terms. At one time
some theorists regarded phenomena brought under these headings as being different from personality—Allport (1937b) defined character as personality evaluated—or as something to
be included within personality—"Temperament refers to the
characteristic phenomena of an individual's emotional nature,
. . . these phenomena being regarded as dependent upon constitutional make-up and therefore largely hereditary in origin"
(Allport, 1937b, p. 54). Surveyors of the field, such as Mac-
Kinnon (1944), had to discuss the boundary problems thus
posed. Today we are spared this necessity because character
and temperament have simply been absorbed into that vast

domain called variables of personality. The question of whether there are clusters or syndromes that deserve one or the other of these names is usually regarded as an empirical rather than a theoretical one. Psychoanalytic theory and practice still make some systematic use of the concept of character, but the typical personality psychologist—if he is interested in such matters— is likely to consider any of the observables here involved under the general heading of ego-functioning.

Intelligence is a more complicated matter. From the point of view of organismic theory of personality, intellectual performance is regarded in the same way as any other performance. One observes consistencies in behavior and hypothesizes underlying regularities of functioning in the personality. One can refer to these regularities as intelligence. On the other hand, in our society much interest attaches to intelligent behavior, and usually we are interested in all its correlates, some of which are certainly not in the personality. Probably for some time, the present practice of measuring and evaluating intellectual performances and then seeking, among other things, their personality correlates will continue. How these correlates are to be conceptualized is an open question. Possibly there are identifiable subsystems that have special roles in intellectual functioning, or it may be that we have to deal here with certain features of the personality organization as a whole.

FIVE

Personality As Field of Inquiry

The field of personality, considered as a domain of research and teaching, has expanded and developed at a phenomenal rate since 1940. In one psychology department—and this is probably not atypical—the first course entitled "Personality" was introduced in 1940. Now that department offers seven courses in the personality area, not including abnormal psychology, individual differences, motivation, or clinical psychology. This elaboration may be slowing down, but it shows no signs of coming to a halt. Moreover, the content of courses changes fairly rapidly in order to keep pace with developments in the field.

Most of the new courses center either upon some method for investigating personality or upon the relations of personality to some other field or order of phenomena. This way of organizing teaching corresponds generally to the prevailing organization of research activity; and although the addition of a new course is usually an expression of the interests of a particular member of a department, the expansion of teaching over the years tends to keep pace with research.

The older courses in the psychology departments were, with respect to method, quite catholic; they made use of the investigations available—case studies, researches involving objective tests of personality, experiments. As the field has expanded and researches have multiplied, it has seemed natural—given the methodological bent of American psychologists—that we should introduce separate courses in case study, personality testing, personality assessment, and experimental psychodynamics. An examination of offerings in university departments that have clinical programs also usually reveals courses in projective techniques and, if the department is large enough, courses concerned with particular techniques, such as the Rorschach test. But these are usually called clinical courses, raising the question of where the personality field stops and clinical psychology begins. This is a difficult matter. It is perhaps enough to suggest that clinical courses accent techniques (and training in their use), whereas personality courses emphasize the substantive aspects of investigations, the line between the two rarely being very clearly drawn. Although one fairly non-controversial way of subdividing the field of personality is according to the method by which data or research results are obtained, it remains debatable how far subdivision and specialization along this line can be carried without resulting in a lamentable fragmentation of the field. Perhaps the limit has already been reached.

Earlier, I observed that preference for a given method tends to be associated with preference for a given theory concerning the nature of personality. Organismic theorists, for example, favor case studies. But the relationship is by no means one to one. Some organismic theorists may prefer experiments in lifelike situations outside the consulting room. Similarly, certain perspectives from which personality may be viewed and certain general approaches to its study, though they have implications for methodology, are not tied to any particular method, nor are they bound to any particular theory.

If one thinks of personality as an organization that exhibits some continuity even as it changes throughout the individual's life, then one may, as we have seen, concentrate (1) on different time spans (or periods or stages) in the existence of the personality, (2) on its changing aspects or on its more enduring features, and (3) on systematic or on historical approaches to explaining its functioning. Divisions of labor according to these several emphases may be noted in teaching and research.

The whole life span is sometimes regarded as a suitable unit for study (Bühler, 1935; Lehman, 1936; Macfarlane, 1960; Murray, 1938, 1949; Rosenzweig, 1955). According to White (1963b), the study of lives has been the major concern of the Harvard Psychological Clinic. Courses in biography or personality as biography sometimes appear among the departmental offerings. More commonly, of course, certain vaguely defined periods of life, such as adolescence or later maturity, get special attention. Such courses or investigations may be concerned primarily with personality, or they may look more broadly at various determinants of certain kinds of behavior or at the effects of environmental factors that become prominent at particular times of life. However, one could quite logically abstract a certain segment of the life span and study the organization of personality in both its changing and enduring aspects during that period. In contrast to investigations or courses directed to the life span or large segments of it, there are, of course, the usual inquiries about the organization of personality as it is found at the time of an experiment or during the course of, for example, a three-day assessment period.

One sometimes encounters nowadays a course in personality change, which attempts to bring together materials from psychotherapy, experiments, and longitudinal studies of development. In contrast to the effort to predict (or forecast) future performances from measures of the presumably more durable traits or features of the personality, a traditional concern of the psychology of individual differences, courses in personality change accent traits more subject to development. The great difficulty with change versus enduringness as the basis for a division in the field of personality is the lack of a good reason why any subsystem of the personality should not be observed with attention both to change and to permanence. On the other hand, a department which teaches the substantive aspects of personality from only the individual differences point of view would seem to have room for a course in personality change.

Courses or texts dealing with personality development are highly varied. Such a course or text may be concerned primarily with a major theory of personality, such as stimulus-response theory, psychoanalysis, or gestalt theory, or with all of these; it may be organized around different periods of life or stages of development, or around different processes or determinants of change; it may accent continuity with the past (enduringness) or new beginnings (change); finally, it may limit itself to either historical or systematic causation. This last distinction has been maintained not only in different approaches to development but in divisions of the field of personality as a whole. Experimental psychodynamics, which took its major inspiration from Lewin's (1935) exposition of systematic causation, was one of the first additions to course offerings in personality. It stood in contrast to the conventional course, which accented consistency in behavior and the diagnosis of persisting tendencies, assuming that what was present in the personality had been learned as a result of past experiences. Although courses on experimental psychodynamics accented the results of controlled investigations, other sources of information were commonly utilized. Time was taken to familiarize the student with such phenomena as substitution, repression, and regression. The division of labor along the line of systematic versus historical causation has been a useful one, and it still makes sense. Today, however, much of the material that used to belong to experimental psychodynamics and personality has been brought into the standard course on motivation, and most students of personality are concerned with both the systematic and the historical causes of the phenomena they observe.

Along with courses on changes in (or methods of studying) personality, departments commonly offer "personality and . . ." courses, a familiar feature not only in psychology, but also in sociology, anthropology, and social welfare departments. The object of such study is the relations of personality to each of the groups of phenomena that adjoin it. In one group of relationships, personality variables are usually in the dependent role. Kluckhohn and Murray (1948) refer to society, culture, and constitution as determinants of personality, and probably not many psychologists would offer serious objection. The student of personality, however, may display his banner before the "and" and in the title of his course ("personality and culture" instead of "culture and personality," as the anthropologist would have it, or "personality and social role" instead of "role determinants of personality," as the sociologist would have it). When one says "personality and physique" or "personality and bodily changes," he suggests that personality may be the independent variable or that the influences of the two domains are mutual at the least, as in the interaction of personality and its social environment. Although personality is more determined than determining in the vast array of studies of personality in relation to cultural, social, physical, and physiological factors, there is another group of "personality and . . ." courses (and investigations) in which personality is rather clearly the determinant, as when psychologists study the relationship between personality and some form (or effect) of behavior—personality and opinion, personality and prejudice, and conformity, and delinquency, and leadership, and so on. Specialization according to the phenomenon with which personality is related is undoubtedly here to stay. It arouses little controversy. The possibilities of differentiation within the domains to which personality is related are very great, and we may anticipate further expansion along this line.

In the organization of research activity, the investigator inevitably limits himself to one or a few conceptually distinct elements or subsystems of the personality. Some of these have achieved sufficient status so that the researcher may identify his activity by reference to the domain to which it belongs— researches in ego-functioning, self-concept, cognitive structures, or mechanisms of defense. In teaching, however, it is extremely rare to divide the labor in this way. In the academic departments we do not find one course on the self-concept and another on conscience and its vicissitudes. The contrast with the state of affairs in psychoanalytic institutes is striking. Here the curriculum, designed largely in accordance with the psychoanalytic theory of personality, contains courses on libido theory, dreams, mechanisms of defense, superego, and so on.

As suggested above, something of this subdivision according to theoretical structure crept into psychology departments under the guise of experimental psychodynamics, where the emphasis was often upon mechanisms rather than upon the traditional contents (needs, attitudes), but this was usually not a frank division according to theoretical structure. A course in psychology of the unconscious may also give special attention to certain hypothetical subsystems rarely treated fully in the standard course on personality—complexes, insatiable needs, unconscious fantasies. On the other hand, a course on the unconscious may be taught from the point of view of general psychology or may occupy itself with an aggregate of isolated abnormal phenomena and not be a course in personality at all.

Resistance in the psychology departments to dividing the teaching of personality according to a theoretical scheme seems in part to express devotion to the prevailing organismic point of view. When one undertakes to present the basic facts and theories of personality, he is likely to experience a strong impulse to deal with the whole thing or to concentrate upon its salient feature, which turns out to be organization. If he takes up theories of personality in turn, it soon appears that

each is an effort to conceptualize the whole—the elements
and their organization. I have taught a course in personality
regularly since 1940. Looking back, I see that it has changed
a great deal. At first it was organized around Murray's need
scheme, then around a psychoanalytic frame of reference, and
in more recent years around a general-systems approach. But
at all times it was a course in personality rather than in some
part or subsystem thereof. Probably such resistance to fragmentation is widespread among personality psychologists.

Perhaps even more important than this resistance to
dividing the personality has been the reluctance among academic psychologists to make the necessary commitment to a
general theoretical scheme and, when such commitments are
made, an inability to achieve the agreement necessary to plan
teaching. This statement is striking testimony to the relative
lack of theoretical development of personality as a field. How
is that development to be achieved? There are obvious advantages to adopting the psychoanalytic frame of reference, with
its rational basis for subdividing the whole personality, but the
wariness of many personality psychologists about premature
structuring, with its threats to objectivity and to freedom in
interpreting events, has not been altogether misplaced. On the
other hand, delay of the development of an acceptable general
theory involves grave danger, for in the absence of such a
theory, the present tendency to organize the field according to
methodologies or relations with other fields will result in serious fragmentation and watering down.

Another way to organize the field, depending neither on
a general theory nor on a particular methodology, is to begin
with the observation that each personality is unique. Although
several authors have included the idea of uniqueness or of
unique adjustments in their definitions of personality, this
argument and the plea for the study of the single case have
been put most forcibly and most persistently by G. W. Allport.
He stated his general position in 1937, and in 1955 and 1961
we find him sticking to his guns. By and large, psychologists
seem to have been rather unimpressed by Allport's argument

and plea. Many have answered him by pointing out that every entity in nature—each part or feature of a person, each event—is unique and that science can proceed only by noting uniformities; that all laws of nature are essentially of a statistical character, being statements about the average of a number of events; that if we can average the responses of a single individual, we may do the same with the responses of many individuals; that the uniqueness of a given personality may be set forth by specifying his position with respect to a number—and not necessarily a very large number—of general traits considered to be normally distributed in a population.

Nevertheless, the notion has persisted that the study of personality should be primarily concerned with the individual, what differentiates him from other individuals, and the ways in which he is rare, if not unique. What is general belongs to general psychology, what is unique may be claimed by personality psychology. Rather curiously, on this point certain general psychologists have made common cause with Allport, with whom they otherwise seem to have little in common.

Meanwhile, psychologists who have been most intimately involved with the study of individual personalities—in personality assessment (for example, MacKinnon, 1952; Murray, 1938; OSS Assessment Staff, 1948; White, 1952), clinical diagnostic studies (for example, Burton and Harris, 1955; Klopfer and Kelley, 1946; Phillipson, 1956; Tomkins, 1947), and psychotherapeutic work (for example, Bullard, 1959; Greenson, 1959; Mowrer, 1953)—have acted as if they had never heard of Allport's recommendation that they concentrate on individual differences or unique organizations. They have generalized. They have supposed that their statements about relationships in the personalities they study—how tensions are managed, defenses are maintained, new experiences are assimilated, and the like—are quite generally true. Indeed, they have supposed that their formulations of individual cases also have some generality, that the pattern of dynamic relationships found to characterize a given individual is very similar to patterns that can be found in other—perhaps many other—individuals. From a methodological point of view, the major criticism of these students of personality has been that they tend to overgeneralize and to suppose, for example, that what is true of neurotics is true of people in general or that what is found in Western cultures is found universally. The uniqueness of the individual, then, has not been the foremost (or even an important) concern of psychologists who have been most involved with the study of individuals.

Allport (1937b) says: "Strictly speaking every adjustment of every person is unique, in time and place, and in quality. In a sense, therefore, this criterion seems redundant. It becomes important, however, in our later discussions of the problem of quantitative variation among individuals in respect to the so-called common traits . . . and is therefore emphasized in the definition" (p. 49). Clearly Allport does not mean that personality determines the individual's unique adjustments, while adjustments that are not unique are determined by something else or some other conditions. Since all adjustments of all individuals are unique, it is indeed redundant to say unique adjustments. Allport, as he says, is preparing the ground for his critique of common traits and for his accent on the concept of ideographic trait. But since all manifestations of all traits are unique, one can make statements about traits only on the basis of uniformities and averages of numerous responses. Most psychologists would probably agree that not all traits exist in all people, that some are far more common than others, and that some are rare. All this is as plain to Allport as it is to anybody else.

The way to understand his position is to put the accent not on uniqueness, but on holism. What Allport most wants to do, as he makes clear in *Becoming* (1955), is to understand the Johnian quality of John's behavior. The way to accomplish this goal is not to study a thousand other people in order to show how unlike them John is; it is rather to study each aspect of John in relation to his whole personality to see how something of John himself is expressed in each segment of his behavior. This is the holistic approach, and a study of Allport's methodological recommendations shows that all of them are consistent with it. His complaints about the usual approach of clinical psychology were boiled down to two in 1955: the universal dimensions employed in the study of personality may be irrelevant to John's personality; and the study of the interrelations of the dimensions has not been carried far enough. Most clinical psychologists, while taking a far less pessimistic view with respect to the possibilities of common traits, would agree that John may have some exceedingly rare traits. As for the second criticism, they would admit it with enthusiasm, urging that the study of the interrelations of dimensions of the person is the most important (and the most difficult) task of psychology.

But—and this is a crucial point—to expose the Johnian quality of John's behavior or to state one's understanding of the vast and complicated structure of his personality is not to say that the Johnian quality of John is not very much like the Willian quality of Will or that certain scientific and practical purposes are not best served by grouping the two individuals. And we say this while granting that John is unique and Will is unique, as everybody else is, and that each is uniquely valuable. As Kluckhohn and Murray (1948, p. 35) neatly state: "Every man is in some respects (1) like all other men, (2) like some other men, (3) like no other man." Psychology has so far been almost entirely concerned with the second point—with the discovery of the ways in which a man or a group of men is like some other men. Of course, we would like to know the ways in which all men are psychologically alike, but obstacles to sampling the whole human race have so far proved insuperable. And in the highly differentiated and complex Western societies in which most psychological research is carried on, differences in age, sex, social class, and subculture loom very large indeed. Still, we can say that among normal adults in Western societies some modes of behavior seem quite general and that in some respects a given man is like a great many others. This statement holds for what is ordinarily called personality functioning as well as for the familiar processes of perception and learning.

Obviously, if one wished to know what to expect under some condition from the whole population of the United States or how to influence that population, as advertisers and propagandists often do, one would do best to use averages.

Much psychological work aimed at the control of behavior is directed to distinctive subgroups of the population. The more humanistic applications of psychology—psychotherapy and counseling, education and correctional work, and child training—are always concerned with the individual. Here the psychologist is guided mainly by knowledge of ways in which the individual is like some others, and the most general principles are not the most helpful ones. Many of them are taken to be general rules, of which the given individual's functioning is a special case. But because each individual is a special case, as study shows, his differences from others in particular functions usually have to be referred to larger organizations in his personality. This organization is, of course, unique. But there is nothing to do about uniqueness—except admire it or perhaps understand and manipulate the conditions that favor it. Any action must be based on knowledge of the conditions under which it will produce a given effect. The conditions with which the psychotherapist or educator primarily deals are to be found in the individual's organized states and processes, which have some generality. It is this generality that makes practical work with individuals possible.

Now that we have sketched various ways of organizing the field of personality, we can take up the perplexing question of how personality is related to general psychology. In 1925 the difference between these two fields was clear. General psychology stressed laboratory studies of the generalized adult mind, abstracting part processes such as learning or perception and studying them in many subjects. It was guided by the waning classical introspectionism or by the still fairly new behaviorism. The whole vast area of molar behavior (particularly motivation) and the personality processes brought over from the clinic (complexes, mechanisms of defense) were left to the personality psychologists. Problems of definition were as acute then as now, but nobody was troubled about his identity as either a personality psychologist or a general psychologist. Each had his own concepts, methods, and assumptions, and the two had very little in common.

Since then, however, the concepts and theories from the dynamic psychology of personality have won wide acceptance. Psychologists in general (Jones, 1957; Lindzey, 1958) have recognized that motivational phenomena and the relations of motivation to other processes, even repression, are just as general as the more familiar phenomena of learning or perception. Thus Hilgard (1949) stated, in his presidential address before the American Psychological Association: "The problems of human motivation and personality belong to all psychologists. The problems of the self-concept are general problems of psychological science" (p. 380).

During the same period, developments in general psychology gave rise to the hope that we were about to achieve a general theory adequate to deal with the whole range of behavior, including the functioning of the personality, of course. Some psychologists felt that theories developed and elaborated on the basis of the intensive study of particular areas of subject matter could be generalized to all behavior. Major examples are Hull's (1943) theory, springing mainly from studies of learning, and gestalt theories, springing mainly from the study of perception (Kofka, 1935; Kohler, 1929).

Of particular significance has been the field theory of Lewin, as set forth in *Dynamic Theory of Personality* (1935). Allport could call this title a misnomer, on the ground that Lewin's theory appeared to be straight general psychology. Allport was most struck, of course, by the absence of any reference to individual differences and of any means for depicting the uniqueness of the individual. Personality psychologists working in the functionalist, or action, tradition wondered what had happened to their familiar variables of personality—instincts, needs, traits, complexes, and the like—which they were in the habit of relating to the past history of the individual. For Lewin, behavior was to be explained systematically, that is, by reference to a field that contained variables in the person and forces in the psychological environment. He wrote that his psychology was deliberately conceived to bring the experimental method to bear upon "such vital problems as those with which psychoanalysis was concerned." He and his associates and followers have produced much research on such problems as anger, altruism, regression, frustration, substitution, and level of aspiration (Barker, Dembo, and Lewin, 1941; Dembo, 1931; Henle, 1942, 1944; Lewin, Dembo, Festinger, and Sears, 1944; Lewin, Lippitt, and White, 1939; Ovsiankina, 1928; Wright, 1942; Zeignarnik, 1927). The point for us here is not only that the "laws" of behavior, for Lewin, were general—thus did not include individual differences—but that the accent on the field had the effect of smudging the traditional boundaries between personality and environment. This blurring of boundaries has meant, for example, that contemporary gestalt psychologists investigate problems from the erstwhile private preserves of personality psychology without feeling any need to mention personality or individual differences at all.

While general psychology has thus been stretching itself to embrace more and more of what used to belong to the personality field, research in personality—most of it informed by the prevailing action and organismic point of view—has brought variables of personality to an increasingly prominent place in the attention of experimentalists in general psychology. Personality psychologists have undertaken hundreds of researches devoted to showing that variables of personality are predictive of individual differences in the performance of laboratory tasks. In recent years, general psychologists have often used the same design; witness a succession of experiments in which scores on the Taylor (1951) anxiety scale have been related to conditioning. Such work has increased the doubt that general laws hold in any detailed way for all people regardless of age, sex, culture, social class, and personality. The theory and experimental work of Brunswik (1943, 1947, 1950), with its assumption of the probabilistic aspect of perceiving, has further cast doubt on the generalizability of our laboratory-derived laws.

The developments mentioned above have brought personality and general psychology closer together and have exposed a great deal of overlapping of the two areas. Many psychologists, unable to enjoy any longer the splendid isolation of the past, have been facing up to the problem of definition. But with their usual flair for disagreement, they have succeeded in taking positions about as far apart as they can get. Some view general psychology as one of several sciences that are propaedeutic to personology, the central science of man. Others regard personality psychology as a branch of general psychology, assuming that the more complex phenomena of personality are ultimately reducible to general psychological laws. Each of these views is worthy of some discussion.

Child (1954, p. 149) has written in favor of the general psychological approach to personality:

The writer has no interest in helping to preserve the integrity of personality study as an isolated entity, welcoming instead the fact that as general psychology becomes more adequate to deal with the whole range of human behavior there is ever less occasion to recognize personality study in the traditional sense as a discipline in any way distinct.

Again, note Hilgard (1953, p. 407):

Personality is saved from being synonymous with general psychology because its reference is to the single individual and to the unique organization of the traits that characterize him and his activity.

These writers are expressing a view that has a long history. Psychology is the study of behavior, and personality is the learned behavior of people, the result of the way in which individuals have adjusted to the world. Of course, people differ widely in what they have learned; each person is indeed unique. But all have learned in accordance with the same general laws, and presumably the functioning or behaving of the personality right now—the assimilation of new experiences, the management of conflicting tensions, and the like—is in accordance with the general laws of psychology. The essential point is that there are no laws of personality functioning apart from the laws of general psychology.

But personality is "saved" from being synonymous with general psychology because of its concern with individual differences and the uniqueness of each person. Thus its natural concern is with the measurement of the learned characteristics of the person, its units of analysis being taken most appropriately from general psychology—motives, perceptions, emotional reactions, and so on. Each individual is uniquely organized; his characteristics are organized in accordance with general psychological laws. This point of view is perhaps most closely associated with representatives of Hull's learning theory, such as Dollard and Miller (1950) and Mowrer (1960), along with Child and Hilgard. It is also expressed by writers not so identified, Stagner (1948), for example.

In a curious way, this view gains strength from Allport's position. He, as we have seen, has been at pains to stress individuality, the unique, as the special province of personality study. Writers such as those just listed have been happy to say, "All right, you can have it," and to cite him in support of their view that general psychology is responsible for the bulk of psychological knowledge, while personality is a fringe domain. They do this despite Allport's views that most so-called general psychology is off the track and can contribute little or nothing to the kind of individuality he means. Of course, Allport himself has contributed to the general psychology of personality development, most notably with his doctrine of functional autonomy (1937b).

Writers who stress the general psychological approach to personality usually regard psychology as a relatively advanced science and seem optimistic about the possibilities of developing (perhaps soon) a general theory adequate to deal with the whole range of human behavior. It is probably no accident that staunch supporters of this view have usually been identified with some particular theoretical system and have perhaps been led to overestimate its potency.

If the essence of the point of view just described is that personality functioning has no laws apart from the laws of general psychology, the essence of the present view is that no psychological laws are truly general if they fail to take personality processes into account. Cattell (1950) gives a strong statement of this position. Not only is study of the total personality necessary for applications in industrial, educational, and clinical psychology—the individual being the same whether he appears in factory, school, or clinic—but

this mandate from applied psychology is less imperative than the corresponding demand from pure psychology for founding all progress in particular fields upon a study of personality. We do not deal with a "perception" or an "emotion" or a "conditioned reflex," but with an organism perceiving or acquiring a conditioned reflex as part of some large pattern or purpose. . . . It is essential to bring fine laboratory instruments to bear in experiments on behavior; but it is a mistake to suppose that laws of learning, or of perception and emotion, can be found that do not take into account the total personality. The study of the total personality is thus the hub from which radiate all more specialized studies, and it is only by turning on this center that they make progress. [p. 2]

Similarly Klein (1951) cites research that provides

ample evidence that purposes, aims, intentions, suffuse the very act of perceiving. All this work challenges the idea of "internal requiredness" or autochthony in the stimulus field, of "field structures" which are so compelling as to have a predestined and universal effect independent of personal intent. It has also

helped to bury the older conception of an autonomous per-
ceptual system which is capable of study apart from the larger
context of the total system of the person, an idea born out of
a myopia to personality theory. [p. 328]

Perhaps the most widely quoted statement of this general point
of view is that of Klein and Krech (1951, p. 11):

The kind of theory we are advocating is one which views all
behavior within the context of the total organism. This is an-
other way of saying that all the processes within the organism
are "adaptive"; each function or behavior serves an organismic
purpose.

And they argue with nice balance that "an adequate personality theory must be a thoroughgoing behavior theory and all
theories of behavior must be personality theories" (p. 11). Part
of the interest attaching to these statements springs from the
fact that Klein and Krech strike many psychologists, as they do
me, as strange bedfellows. Klein has long been identified with
personality research, particularly with the kind of investigation
that relates individual differences in laboratory performances
to the functioning of personality, while Krech is a general psychologist, long an exponent of gestalt psychology and, more
recently, of a general-systems theory. It is as if Krech were
saying, "An adequate personality theory must be a thoroughgoing behavior theory," and Klein were completing the sen-
tence with "and all theories of behavior must be personality
theories."

Although these writers represent the general psychological approach to personality, particularly in what was just ascribed to Krech, the general intent of their paper is to support
the organismic point of view as against classical reductionism.
These writers are frankly and warmly holistic, quoting with
approval von Bertalanffy on the point that preponderance of
vital processes and mechanisms must be understood as helping
to maintain the whole.

Perhaps I should point out that on the battleground of holism versus reductionism, Klein and Krech are late arrivals. Among psychologists, probably the most important exponent of the organismic point of view is Murray. Many psychologists have flirted with the organismic outlook—as many still do—but Murray has been married to it. He has stated the position consistently since the late 1930s, has organized large-scale researches in accordance with it, and has devised a methodology which, more than any other, has some promise of dealing adequately with its implications. This statement is not intended to belittle the general importance of gestalt psychology or of the holistic thinkers who carry on in the tradition of European thought (Angyal, 1941; Goldstein, 1939; Stern, 1938), but rather to stress the fact that Murray, unlike most of the holists, was willing to separate parts from the whole by abstraction and get on with the business of investigation—thus his importance for American psychology. Gestalt psychology has rarely been involved in intensive investigations of personality. Psychoanalysis, particularly in its European versions, has been implicitly holistic all the time, but its spokesmen have seldom made systematic statements of this position, or if they have, they have not had much influence on psychologists.

Murray's (1938) statement of the organismic point of view follows:

The organism is from the beginning a whole, from which the parts are derived by self-differentiation. The whole and its parts are mutually related, the whole being as essential to an understanding of the parts as the parts are to an understanding of the whole. (This is a statement of the organismal theory.) Theoretically it should be possible to formulate for any moment the "wholeness" of an organism; or in other words, to state in what respect it is acting as a unit. [p. 39]

Murray says he takes his wording from Russel (1916), who in turn has stated the organismal viewpoint of Ritter (1919). Murray continues (p. ix):

We were accustomed to conceive of personality as a temporal integrate of mutually dependent processes (variables) developing in time, and from this conception it follows that a large number of determining variables as well as their relations must be recognized and approximately measured if one is to give an adequate interpretation—analysis and synthesis—of a singe human event. . . . This conclusion led to our first important decision, which was: that all experimenters should use one and the same group of subjects. Each worker continued as before with his own problem, but under the new plan he had the findings of other observers to aid him in the interpretation of his results.

"His own problem" often included the experimental attack on some general psychological problem—emotional conditioning, sensorimotor learning, repressing, cheating, reacting to frustration. Holt, Klein, and others of the New York University Research Center for Mental Health and at the Institute of Personality Assessment and Research at the University of California under the direction of MacKinnon have followed this general approach.

If personality and general psychology overlapped so much as the above discussion would seem to indicate, we would have to face the question of whether they are to be separated at all and, if so, in accordance with what principles. However, the above statements about the generality of psychological laws and about the inclusiveness of the organismic point of view are programatic and not at all descriptive of the present state of affairs in psychology.

The accomplishments of general psychology, measured against the task of dealing scientifically with the whole range of human behavior, are not impressive. General psychology can predict, to a degree somewhat better than chance, the average response of a group of individuals to a variety of stimuli or situations, but it is rather far from being able to predict the response of any one individual. General psychologists seem often to mistake intentions for accomplishments and the capacity to lecture on what science is or ought to be for the capacity to produce scientific knowledge. When it comes to slightly complicated practical problems, general psychology has rarely got beyond a ratification of common sense. The gap between the academic psychology of the laboratory and the practical psychology of psychotherapy is still so large that workers in the two fields seem to be in different realms of discourse. The remark of Richards that psychology had so far managed to say vaguely and obscurely what everybody knew already is still applicable. But he added that here and there new light had crept in. Occasionally it continues to creep in. But scientific general psychology with a bearing on human behavior remains little more than a bright and hopeful promise. Advances in general psychology have been expressed most clearly in the increased willingness of general psychologists to attack more complicated problems. But the effects of these advances have not yet been very sharply reflected in the teaching of general psychology.

As for the organismic point of view, it wins its way slowly. The 1951 paper by Klein and Krech suggests that it has made headway since Murray wrote in 1938, but their call for radical revisions in general psychological research and teaching has fallen largely upon deaf ears; psychologists have continued doing what they were doing. The organismic approach still encounters direct opposition. For example, one of the outstanding researches expressing the new upsurge of the organismic point of view was presented in *Personality Through Perception* by Witkin and others (1953). Although Murphy (1953) called it "an extraordinary achievement" in bringing the process of perception into relation with the entire personality of the perceiver, the approach was severely criticized by Postman (1955), who was inclined to throw it out on methodological grounds and who urged that his fellow academic psychologists forget such morbid personality stuff and concentrate on something fundamental (such as the mechanism of perception). No doubt Postman speaks here for a great many academic psychologists—perhaps the majority.

Again, the realistic supporters of the organismic view have to admit the necessity of abstracting parts from the whole, even the necessity of studying part functions in relative isolation. They have been able only to urge, as did Murray (1938), that the psychologist in his experimental work "recognize that he is observing a part of an operating totality and that this totality, in turn, is but a small temporal segment of a personality" (p. 4). Psychologists have been realistic enough to make a virtue of a necessity; after a nod in the direction of totality, they have gone on doing what they found interesting and rewarding. Even the personality psychologists have not been very organismic as far as their researches are concerned. They have usually been content to use a few variables of personality as predictors of performance in some situations and, like general psychologists, have been happy if they can find statistically significant relationships between averages for groups.

However, limitations upon organismic research have been dictated largely by circumstances. Projects such as that described in *Personality Through Perception* are expensive and difficult to organize. The lone researcher or the graduate student looking for a thesis problem is in a poor position to manage more than a handful of personality variables, and he is almost bound to settle for a design closer to the traditional academic experimental one than to anything truly organismic. The experimental approach still carries such prestige in psychology—is so often regarded as the only road to salvation—that many workers who might otherwise probe deeply into personality choose the method rather than the problem and thus are more at home with their general psychological colleagues than with the honor-bright personologists. Promotions in the university departments depend upon publications; and a short paper based on the experimental manipulation of two or three variables is the most practical vehicle of communication—that, or a textbook or compilation that accords with the prevailing views of what is sound. Only the most secure older psychologist is in a position to embark on a project that may involve two or three years without publication. Many clinical students have been badgered enough by the academic psychologists of their departments—and attracted enough by the rewards of their internships—so that they spend as little time as possible in the department and more time in the clinic, where they fraternize with psychiatrists and become increasingly alienated from academic psychology, cut off from a setting or life space well calculated to inspire or stimulate research.

This situation, among others, leads one to imagine that an anthropologist who read Sapir's article (1934) on personality and then went off on a field trip, renewing his acquaintance with the culture of psychology in 1970, would not feel like a total stranger. He would note that Freud, Jung, and Adler, to whom Sapir devoted the most space, were still the subjects of the first chapters of Lindzey and Hall's standard text (1965). Noting (probably with some wry humor) that the behaviorists and the dynamicists were still at it, he might say to himself, "This is where I came in." Soon, however, he would note that some changes had occurred. He would probably be pleased to discover that personality is now thought of less as a structure of reactivity essentially fixed by the age of two or three—the "psychiatric" definition favored by Sapir—and more as a structure that always interacts with, and is for a long time developed by, social and cultural stimuli. As he looked further, our returning native would begin to be impressed by subtle modifications of theory, including the psychoanalytic version, by strenuous efforts to develop concepts linked more closely to behavior, and by the outpouring of empirical studies. Basically, the field of personality has been developing in five ways.

First, in an important sense, the trend of the discipline, as of the city, is toward a disconcerting sprawl. The field of personality has expanded in all directions, and of the many different voices heard from that field, none can be called dominant. The present is not a time of grand theory. The major theoretical systems current now were all developed before 1950 and most of them date from the 1930s or before. Most of the writers in Lindzey and Hall (1965) and in Sahakian (1965) are still expanding and developing their systems but on foundations laid down much earlier. Personality theorists today seem much more aware of the complexity of personality than was the case in the 1920s, when it was possible to develop a system around a few simple and sovereign ideas. This is an age not of treatises by one man but of the symposium and the collection of essays on a single specialized topic.

Specialization is a natural consequence of expansion. The time has long since passed when a man could be acquainted with all of psychology; today he can hardly keep abreast of developments in personality psychology. A social scientist who turned to the *Psychological Abstracts* in search of information about personality would find little that he was tempted to read. An educator interested in the topic of learning in relation to personality development would discover not one but a variety of theories of learning—and of learning particular kinds of content and of learning in particular situations.

An educated layman, examining the field of personality today, might be impressed by the multiplicity of possibly fruitful approaches, but he would probably be shocked by the spectacle of so much research whose sole link to humanly meaningful issues is a faith in eventual synthesis based upon a naively misappropriated model of science. Many psychologists say that the need today is for empirical work on the hypotheses that have been accumulating over the years and for the generation of elegant theories and of testable hypotheses from the rather grandiose conceptualizations of the past. Others, however, add that the field of personality also requires some resolution, or at least clarification, of the major differences in the philosophy which governs strategies of research as well as theory.

Second, the conflict between behavior theorists and theorists of the dynamic-organismic persuasion exhibits a certain alternation in which now one side and now the other gains the ascendency. In the 1920s the new behaviorism rose to ascendency in American psychology. In the 1930s, however, ideas brought from Europe began a great ferment in American psychology. Freud's psychoanalysis (and other schools of analytic thought, such as those represented by Adler, Fromm, and Horney), gestalt psychology, topological psychology, general-systems theory, and native dynamic theories (such as the one advanced by Murray)—all of these combined to compose an effective opposition to behaviorism. By the end of World War II, a dynamic-organismic approach was clearly dominant within the psychology of personality. In the late 1940s and early 1950s, systems theory, holistic views of personality, and the concepts of self and ego came very much to the fore in the conversation as well as in the research of psychologists; Shakow, taking stock of psychology at the end of the 1950s, could note, as a major trend, "increasing attention to molar studies, accompanied by a diligent search for methods to handle the organized complexity involved" (Shakow and Rapaport, 1964, p. 197).

In the early 1950s, however, a marked change began. Personality oriented clinical psychology, which had expanded dramatically after World War II in response to practical needs and with the help of funds from the Federal government, began to rest on its laurels or paused to consolidate its gains, and behavioristically oriented experimental psychology began to dominate the academic departments. Organized psychology split so profoundly that some talked of organizing clinical psychology in its own department or school. Cronbach (1963), in his presidential address before the American Psychological Association in 1957, gave a sort of official recognition to the split by speaking of the "two disciplines of scientific psychology." One group preferred the experimental method of investigation; another, the correlational—which is one way to express the major theoretical (or perhaps ideological) division we are concerned with here. Cronbach called for a confluence of the two disciplines, but although he offered positive suggestions toward that end, it still does not appear to be in sight.

Meanwhile, research on holistic concepts has been curtailed. No fresh attempts, comparable to that of Dollard and Miller (1950), to translate Freudian ideas into the language of stimulus-response reinforcement theory have been made. Research stimulated by the ideas of Lewin has fallen into a re-

cession as his hypotheses are called not researchable because
the concepts are too remote from anything observable. This
contention, however, has not prevented Lewin's students from
producing a stream of experimental studies on such topics as
anger, regression, conflict, ego involvement, and level of aspiration. Like other holistic theorists, Lewin is a victim of the
times; his ideas, according to Hilgard (1963), remain unassimi-
lated to prevailing theories.

Stagner (1965) has stern words for his colleagues in clinical psychology, many of whom, he says, have abandoned the
effort to understand the whole person in favor of the blindly
empirical research so fashionable in graduate schools. Disagree-
ing with Loevinger (1965), who suggests, sympathetically, that
research inspired by holistic theory may not be able to meet
current standards in psychological experimentation, Stagner
accuses clinical psychologists of neglecting sound research strategies, such as profile analysis and Stephenson's (1953) Q sort,
merely because they are necessarily cumbersome and do not
promise a quick payoff.

When the chips are down psychologists seem still to
have the will to stick together and to remain, for certain practical purposes, one discipline, but American psychologists do
not feel any great pressure toward integration of their theories.
Curiosity about people and the demands of practice will probably lead to another resurgence of dynamic-organismic psychology, but this change will not necessarily bring a confluence
with stimulus-response psychology, for the renewal of interest
in behavior therapy suggests that a polarization has occurred
and may continue.

Third, inspired perhaps by developments in anthropology and sociology, psychologists show a greatly increased
awareness of and concern with the social determinants of personality development and with interactions of personality structures and the contemporary social environment. They generally
agree that virtually all the distinguishable features of personality are correlated with features of the cultural (or social)
environment of the individual's remote or recent past. Indeed,

one may well wonder whether biological factors have not been too much downgraded and neglected. The accent on the social is reflected in the appearance of new personality variables such as role dispositions, interpersonal reaction systems, and social values. Collaboration between personality psychology and the social sciences is a two-way street; for several decades anthropologists have made much use of personality theory, particularly Freudian theory, and historians and other specialists in the humanities show signs of an increasing awareness of their need for a sophisticated understanding of personality (for example, Cohn, 1961). Sociology, concerned with being a pure science, with empirical laws of group functioning, still tends to be somewhat skittish about psychology. Nevertheless, the over-all picture suggests that the prospects for a genuine articulation of personality theory and social theory are good.

Fourth, recent years have seen rising interest in cognitive variables such as cognitive structures, ideologies, and belief systems. In academic psychology cognitive structures are seen not only as expressions of the individual's striving but as motives in their own right or as functions that may develop independently of motives. In psychoanalysis, as we have seen, the new ego psychology places various cognitive functions in the ego, which is considered to have its own independent origins and course of development. These developments are part of a current emphasis on the distinctively human (as opposed to the animal) in man. We may expect the current interest in cognitive variables to continue, along with research on dynamic elements such as needs or impulses. Despite some effective criticism of tension-reduction formulas, the concept of striving remains the major organizing principle in personality theory, and dynamic elements have thus remained the most generally favored personality variables.

Finally, Freudian psychoanalytic theories gained greatly in acceptability after 1935 and are still in relatively good standing. Although few of Freud's physicalistic analogies have survived, save among slavish adherents within what is called official psychoanalysis, everyone in the intellectual community except some stimulus-response psychologists has generally accepted long since the essential and distinctively psychoanalytic ideas of the plasticity of motives and of the dynamic unconscious.

Psychoanalytic ideas do not excite the interest today that they did in the late 1940s. At that time arrangements were being made for psychologists to be psychoanalyzed, psychoanalysts were finding places in university departments, and psychoanalytic research was being supported. In expressing disappointment that the promise of those years has not been realized, some sympathetic observers have wondered whether the decline of interest does not reflect a weakness in the theory. In the early 1950s, however, there was a general reaction, noted above, against holistic theories in general; as one result, only a handful of psychologists were psychoanalyzed, grants for research went to psychoanalysts who were not well trained in methods, and beachheads in university departments were not extended. In any event, the objective study of psychoanalytic concepts and theories continued; psychoanalytically oriented texts in personality (for example, Sarnoff, 1962) are used in university departments, and excellent theoretical work is being done today by psychologists such as Holt (1962), Klein (1956), Loevinger (1965, 1970), Madison (1961), Tomkins (1961), and White (1963a), who are friendly to psychoanalysis and who typically take some vague Freudian formulation and make it the object of clarifying systematic treatment.

In the light of these trends, a merger of personality psychology and general psychology does not seem imminent. Despite an unmistakable trend toward closeness and integration, the traditional divergence in respect to concepts, methods, points of view, and interests is still very much with us. Still, the trend toward integration promises to continue by fits and starts, and it is appropriate to peer into the future in a paper of this sort. Moreover, recent thinking about the general psychology approach to personality and the personological approach to general psychology is sufficiently advanced so that the question of how the two fields should be related in an ideal world is an intellectually intriguing one.

If the organismic point of view came to be universally held, what would the relations of general psychology and personality psychology be? According to the above statements of this point of view, one could no longer say that one kind of psychology was more general than the other or that they differed with respect to the kinds of behavior studied. Since there would be just one psychology, a psychology of persons, both personality psychologists and general psychologists would perform the same kinds of researches, those directed to the exposure of the mutual relations of part and whole processes and to the formulation of organismic laws.

The teaching of psychology, also profoundly modified, might well be modeled after clinical teaching in medicine, which accents the patient rather than particular organ systems taken singly and in turn. Students would be introduced to psychology by means of the case study, starting with cases in which all (or as many as possible) of the person's processes had already been studied by appropriate techniques and seeking an integration of the whole. At the next stage, the students and their instructors would engage in research, all hands studying the same group of subjects throughout the several years of a graduate course. Students would take turns with different procedures or methods—those most appropriate to the study of different processes—while all seminars would be in the nature of staff conferences.

What is wrong with this picture? Perhaps nothing is wrong essentially, but it invites the same response as do all holistic schemes: "This is all very well, but there must be analysis, there must be concentration on complicated part processes, and hence there must be divisions of labor." Cut the pie we must, but in starting with a holistic orientation, we may hope to gain some increase in the rationality or some decrease in the arbitrariness with which we make the cuts.

The organismic point of view does not say merely that part functions, such as learning or perception, depend upon the larger personality systems within which they are embedded; it says that parts and wholes are mutually related. Thus, a student of ego-functioning, let us say, must both consider how such functioning depends upon the organization of the whole personality and analyze ego-functioning in terms of processes operating at a lower level. This way of approaching psychological problems becomes clear enough to the personologist when he is called upon to explain the functioning of social groups. Although inclined to favor analysis in terms of the personalities of the constituent members, as a true holist he is not surprised or put off if a social theorist reminds him that personality itself is not fully revealed until the individual is seen in the context of the social group.

Although classical reductionism allows no place for holistic laws, the process does not work the other way around; holism does not eliminate the necessity for certain reductive activity, for the explanation of complex phenomena by reference to interactions of processes at the next lower level. Thus, for example, we may go from the behavior of social organizations to the personalities of the constituent members, from personalities to motives and emotions, from motives and emotions to conditioning, and from conditioning to phenomena of isolated nerve fibers. From this point of view, it is hard to see how analysis at one level can be regarded as more legitimate than analysis at the others. The student of conditioning who is somewhat contemptuous of the vague globalism of the student of emotion can be regarded in the same way by a student of the action of the nervous system. The scientist who prefers a given level of analysis should use concepts consistent with what is known at lower levels, remembering that the object of reduction is to make a better synthesis possible, to increase our understanding of the wholes that are just as "real" as their parts.

It is difficult to meet these requirements, but the direction of progress seems clear enough. Personality psychology traditionally has maintained a certain separateness by concerning itself primarily with relatively gross units of analysis—traits, motives, attitudes, complexes, and the like. Its inferences concerning these psychophysical systems in the individual have been based primarily upon the observation of molar behavior. So long as personality psychology is concerned with the whole person or with a person's life during some fairly long span of time or, for that matter, with the development of a humanistic or practically useful psychology, units of analysis as gross as those mentioned would seem to be a necessity. One may hope, however, that personality psychology will eventually develop a set of terms more adequate than the present ones—terms at once more consistent with the psychology of conditioning, perception, emotion, and the like, and more appropriate to a consideration of the individual as a unit in the social system.

The general psychologist most characteristically devotes himself to a level of analysis somewhere between nervous functioning and the gross units of the personality psychologist, trying to find general laws to which complex phenomena may be reduced and trying to maintain his independence of physiology. Assuming a continuation of this trend in general psychology toward concern with more complex phenomena and the use of larger analytic categories, we should expect the personality psychologist to make room by moving a few steps further to the left. If general psychologists, following Hilgard's (1949) recommendation, are going to study the Freudian mechanisms in relation to the self, we should expect the personality psychologist happily to study the self in relation to still larger subsystems of the personality. And similarly with respect to the time span covered by the behavior under study. If general psychologists are going to study the achievement drive in relation to performance in a series of experimental tasks lasting, for example, a week, they have to take but a step in order to study the achievement drive in relation to performances in natural situations lasting through several years of school. In this case, we should expect the personality psychologist to direct his attention to still larger intervals of time, even to the whole life span.

In short, it is impossible to see how differences in levels of analysis are to be dispensed with or why there should not be divisions of labor. Such divisions are bound to involve differences in method. The general psychologist, in search of detailed information about some particular function which he abstracts from the whole and analyzes with the use of finer categories, may be able to limit himself to rigorous tests and experimental procedures. If the personality psychologist should insist on covering more ground, however, on working to embrace the true totality of the personality of the moment or of the life span, he will of course have to rely, as in the past, upon the case history and upon such procedures as the interview and projective techniques, which aim at comprehensiveness. Thus we are bound to have specialists, and—given the inclination of American psychologists to become attached to their methods—we should expect less than perfect understanding among the specialists working at different levels and in various subregions.

As for what the general psychologist may single out for intensive study, perhaps we should not expect or desire any complete break with tradition. It has been stated that personality psychology and general psychology cannot be separated on the basis of the kinds of behavior they study. This is not to say that they may not concentrate upon different kinds of relationships among the kinds of behavior. When I was a graduate student in 1930, I was presented with the following schema in a psychophysics course. S stood for stimulus, NS for nervous system, C for consciousness, and B for behavior. These were

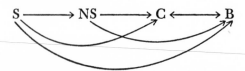

the data available to the psychologist, and his proper study was the relationships among them. Each of these domains of data obviously covers much territory, and one could study relationships obtaining within each (although in this case he would have to limit himself to consciousness and behavior in order to remain within the realm of psychology). For that matter one could, following Brunswik (1950), divide the stimulus and the behavior domains into their proximal and distal and their molecular and molar aspects and study the relationships of these subdivisions. Psychology has come a long way since 1930, but we can hardly claim that we know as much about such relationships as we would like or that further information about them may not be obtained by the traditional procedure of abstracting them from their organismic context. The kind of psychology that attends to such matters may not be very general, but it is certainly not personality psychology.

From time to time interest attaches to a particular variable within one or another of the domains just indicated and to the discovery of all its correlates. If, for example, we are interested in all the correlates of a certain perceiving behavior, we of course study this behavior in relation to numerous variables of personality—attitudes, motives, types of ego organization, and the like—but we also look for correlates in the stimulus field, in the nervous system, in the cultural background of the subject, and so on. In these latter cases, we would most certainly be outside the field of personality psychology. Investigations of this kind are common in social psychology; for example, in work that makes no mention of personality, conforming behavior has been shown to be related to a variety of situational, social, and cultural factors (Allport, 1934; Asch, 1956; Helmreich and Collins, 1968; Newcomb, 1958; Sherif, 1936). In addition, interest often centers quite legitimately upon all the kinds of response or upon the most common response in a given population (or, hopefully, in people in general) to some particular stimulus or stimulus situation.

The great difficulty for general psychology is that the general laws so much admired and so eagerly sought are never very general. On the contrary, they are usually quite specific. The experimentalist, acting in accordance with his ideal of exactitude and limiting himself to variables that can be measured with precision, ignores or controls so many other relevant variables that his final result—a statistically significant relationship between factor A and factor B—is usually of extremely limited generality. To take an example, it is now well known that there are sex differences in the mechanisms of perceiving (Witkin, 1953). Where the experimentalist on perception ignores this fact, as he has usually done in the past, and averages the responses of males and females, we can be sure only that no subject responds as the average says. If, on the other hand, the experimenter takes account of sex differences and limits himself to subjects of one sex or the other, the generality of his findings declines sharply. We have every reason to believe that what is true of sex is also true of various other factors, including social-group memberships and culture, as well as personality—so that all we can say for most of our so-called general psychological propositions is that they are probably true of some people. The dilemma is compounded by the fact that the highest degrees of generality tend to go with the lowest level of analysis. Indeed, the bulk of our most cherished general laws are not truly psychological at all, but rather psychophysiological, and the psychologist who feels he must do something basic still tends to move ever closer to physiology. When this is done without attention to how these basic processes articulate with those on higher levels, it amounts to a flight from the persistent problems of psychology.

Our consideration of the relations of personality and general psychology has led to the conclusion that these two fields do not differ essentially with respect to the behavior they study or to the generality of the propositions they seek to demonstrate. Both are properly interested in general laws governing the relations of behavior and the organization of personality. But so vast and complex are the phenomena involved that we cannot hope to avoid analysis on different levels or the singling out of particular processes for intensive study. Some of these processes involve relationships other than those of the behavior-personality variety and as such fall well outside any psychology of personality. Attention to different levels of analysis and concentration upon particular processes or relationships naturally require much differentiation and specialization in method.

The question naturally arises whether increased under-

standing and perhaps increased coordination of effort are possible among psychologists in general. As we have seen, a natural
methodological consequence of the organismic point of view is,
as Murray (1938) proposed, that all experimenters within a
given institute or department should employ the same group
of subjects, each observer using the findings of the others to
aid him in the interpretation of his results. This suggestion was
published in 1938 after some years of trial at the Harvard Psychological Clinic. Within this general methodological scheme,
psychologists could use techniques ranging all the way from the
most open-ended psychodiagnostic devices to rigorous experimental procedures. Yet the suggestion has rarely been acted
upon. Why? The reasons have as much to do with the social
psychology of the professions—with attitudes and values and
traditions—as with fundamental differences in theory.

A study of our professional behavior may well reveal as
one of its most troublesome features the utopianism of so many
of our experimentalists and general theorists. It is a paradox,
as ingenious as one may hope to find, that while our so-called
hardheaded psychologists were terrorizing the clinicians and
personality researchers by their righteous insistence upon exactitude, experimental rigor, and the like, they themselves were
moved by the wildest dreams of all-embracing theoretical structures or general laws that would hold for all animals in all
times and places. Utopian is the word because so far all such
schemes and most such general laws have fallen to pieces as
soon as they were confronted with the realities of human life,
their adherents meanwhile assuming a role analogous to that
of social reformers who are forever concocting plans for saving
humanity but who don't like "folks." It would be a considerable aid to understanding if these zealots were to refrain from
advancing their particular schemes and ways of doing things as
if they were science itself and from acting as if what circum-
stance forces them to do was a chosen path to salvation instead.

Personality psychology, by no means free of the strains
that beset psychology in general, has for some time tended to
split into a rigorous experimental branch and a sort of clinical,

holistic branch. In the former, there seems often to be an inclination to win acceptance by imitating the prevalent style of
research in psychology; in the latter, an element of defensive
withdrawal and a too hasty conclusion that academic psychology
has nothing to offer. One hopes that personality psychologists
who are tempted by the first alternative will honor the distinctive challenge of their field and that those of the latter inclination will realize that there is no way to do without basic
psychology.

Bibliography

ADAMS, D. *The Anatomy of Personality.* Garden City, N.Y.: Doubleday, 1954.

ADELSON, J. "Personality." In P. H. Mussen and M. R. Rosenzweig (Eds.), *Annual Review of Psychology.* Palo Alto, Calif.: Annual Reviews, 1969.

ADORNO, T. W., FRENKL-BRUNSWIK, E., LEVINSON, D. J., and SANFORD, R. N. *The Authoritarian Personality.* New York: Harper and Row, 1950.

ALFERT, E. "An Idiographic Analysis of Personality Differences Between Reacting to a Vicariously Experienced Threat and Reactions to a Direct Threat." *Journal of Experimental Research in Personality,* 1967, 2, 200–207.

ALLPORT, F. H. "The J-Curve Hypothesis of Conforming Behavior." *Journal of Social Psychology,* 1934, 5, 141–183.

ALLPORT, F. H. *Theories of Perception and the Concept of Structure.* New York: Wiley, 1955.

145

ALLPORT, G. W. "The Personalistic Psychology of William Stern." *Character and Personality*, 1937, *5*, 231–246. (a)

ALLPORT, G. W. *Personality: A Psychological Interpretation.* New York: Holt, Rinehart, and Winston, 1937. (b)

ALLPORT, G. W. "The Ego in Contemporary Psychology." *Psychological Review*, 1943, *50*, 451–478.

ALLPORT, G. W. *Becoming.* New Haven, Conn.: Yale University Press, 1955.

ALLPORT, G. W. "The Open System in Personality Theory." *Journal of Abnormal and Social Psychology*, 1960, *61*, 301–310.

ALLPORT, G. W. *Pattern and Growth in Personality.* New York: Holt, Rinehart, and Winston, 1961.

ALLPORT, G. W. "The Trend in Motivational Theory" (1953). In M. Mednick and S. A. Mednick (Eds.), *Research in Personality.* New York: Holt, Rinehart, and Winston, 1963.

ANGYAL, A. *Foundations for a Science of Personality.* Cambridge, Mass.: Harvard University Press, 1941.

ASCH, S. E. *Social Psychology.* Englewood Cliffs, N.J.: Prentice-Hall, 1952.

ASCH, S. E. "Studies of Independence and Submission to Group Pressure: I. A Minority of One Against a Unanimous Majority." *Psychological Monographs*, 1956, *70* (416).

ASHBY, R. W. *Design for a Brain.* New York: Wiley, 1952.

BALINT, M. "On Genital Love." *International Journal of Psycho-Analysis*, 1948, *29*, 34–40.

BARKER, R. G., DEMBO, T., and LEWIN, K. "Frustration and Regression: An Experiment with Young Children." *University of Iowa Studies in Child Welfare*, 1941, *18* (1).

BARKER, R. G., WRIGHT, B. A., and GONICK, M. R. *Adjustment to Physical Handicap and Illness: A Survey of the Social Psychology of Physique and Disability.* New York: Social Science Research Council, 1946.

BARKER, R. G., and WRIGHT, H. F. "Psychological Ecology and the Problem of Psychosocial Development." *Child Development*, 1949, *20*, 131–143.

BARKER, R. G., and WRIGHT, H. F. *Midwest and Its Children: The Psychological Ecology of an American Town.* New York: Harper and Row, 1955.

BARRON, F. "Complexity-Simplicity as a Personality Dimension." *Journal of Abnormal and Social Psychology*, 1953, *48*, 163–172. (a)

BARRON, F. "An Ego-Strength Scale Which Predicts Response to Psychotherapy." *Journal of Consulting Psychology*, 1953, *17*, 327–333. (b)

BARRON, F. "Some Personality Correlates of Independence of Judgment." *Journal of Personality*, 1953, *21*, 287–297. (c)

BARRON, F. *Personal Soundness in University Graduate Students*. Berkeley, Calif.: University of California Press, 1954.

BARTLETT, F. C. *Remembering*. New York: Cambridge, 1932.

BERGMANN, G. "Theoretical Psychology." In C. P. Stone (Ed.), *Annual Review of Psychology*. Palo Alto, Calif.: Annual Reviews, 1953.

BERGMANN, G. *Philosophy of Science*. Madison, Wis.: University of Wisconsin Press, 1957.

BERGMANN, G., and SPENCE, K. W. "Operationism and Theory Construction." In M. H. Marx (Ed.), *Psychological Theory*. New York: Macmillan, 1951.

BERTOCCI, P. A. "The Psychological Self, the Ego and Personality." *Psychological Review*, 1945, *52*, 91–99.

BETTELHEIM, B. "Individual and Mass Behavior in Extreme Situations." *Journal of Abnormal and Social Psychology*, 1943, *38*, 417–425.

BLOCK, J., and BLOCK, J. "An Investigation of the Relationship Between Intolerance of Ambiguity and Ethnocentrism." *Journal of Personality*, 1951, *19*, 303–311.

BLOOM, B. S. *Stability and Change in Human Characteristics*. New York: Wiley, 1964.

BOTT, E. *Family and Social Network*. London: Tavistock, 1957.

BRAND, H. "The Contemporary Status of the Study of Personality." In H. Brand (Ed.), *The Study of Personality*. New York: Wiley, 1954.

BRIDGMAN, P. W. *The Logic of Modern Physics*. New York: Macmillan, 1927.

BRONFENBRENNER, U. "Toward an Integrated Theory of Personality." In R. R. Blake and G. V. Ramsey (Eds.), *Perception: An Approach to Personality*. New York: Ronald, 1951.

BROWN, D. "Personality, College Environments, and Academic Productivity." In N. Sanford (Ed.), *The American College*. New York: Wiley, 1962.

BROWNFAIN, J. J. "Stability of the Self Concept as a Dimension of Personality." *Journal of Abnormal and Social Psychology*, 1952, *47*, 597–606.

BRUNER, J. S. "Personality Dynamics and the Process of Perceiving." In R. R. Blake and G. V. Ramsey (Eds.), *Perception: An Approach to Personality*. New York: Ronald, 1951.

BRUNER, J. S., and GOODMAN, C. "Value and Need as Organizing Factors in Perception." *Journal of Abnormal and Social Psychology*, 1947, *42*, 33–44.

BRUNER, J. S., and others. *Contemporary Approaches to Cognition*. Cambridge, Mass.: Harvard University Press, 1957.

BRUNSWIK, E. "Organismic Achievement and Environmental Probability." *Psychological Review*, 1943, *50*, 255–272.

BRUNSWIK, E. *Systematic and Representative Design of Psychological Experiments*. Berkeley, Calif.: University of California Press, 1947.

BRUNSWIK, E. "The Conceptual Framework of Psychology." In Vol. 1 of *International Encyclopedia for the Unification of Science*. Chicago: University of Chicago Press, 1950.

BÜHLER, C. "The Curve of Life as Studied in Biographies." *Journal of Applied Psychology*, 1935, *19*, 405–409.

BÜHLER, C. "Maturation and Motivation." *Personality: Symposia on Topical Issues*, 1951, *1*, 184–211.

BÜHLER, K. *Die geistige Entwicklung des Kindes*. (4th ed.) Jena: Gustav Fischer, 1924.

BULLARD, D. M. (Ed.) *Psychoanalysis and Psychotherapy: Selected Papers of Frieda Fromm-Reichmann*. Chicago: University of Chicago Press, 1959.

BURTON, A., and HARRIS, R. E. (Eds.). "Case Histories in Clinical and Abnormal Personality." In Vol. 2 of *Clinical Studies of Personality*. New York: Harper and Row, 1955.

BURWEN, L. S., and CAMPBELL, D. T. "The Generality of Attitudes Toward Authority and Nonauthority Figures." *Journal of Abnormal and Social Psychology*, 1957, *54*, 24–31.

CANTRIL, H. "The Place of Personality in Social Psychology." *Journal of Psychology*, 1947, *24*, 19–56.

CARLSON, R. "Stability and Change in the Adolescent's Self-Image." *Child Development*, 1965, *36*, 659–666.

CARTWRIGHT, D. "Lewinian Theory as a Contemporary Systematic Framework." In Vol. 2 of S. Koch (Ed.), *Psychology: A Study of a Science*. New York: McGraw-Hill, 1959.

CATTELL, R. B. *Personality*. New York: McGraw-Hill, 1950.

CATTELL, R. B. "Personality Theory Growing from Multivariate Quantitative Research." In Vol. 2 of S. Koch (Ed.), *Psy-*

chology: A Study of a Science. New York: McGraw-Hill, 1959.

CATTELL, R. B., and CROSS, P. "Comparison of the Ergic and Self-Sentiment Structures Found in Dynamic Traits by R- and P-Techniques." *Journal of Personality*, 1952, *21*, 250–270.

Center for the Study of Higher Education, University of California. "Omnibus Personality Inventory: Research Manual." Berkeley, Calif., 1962.

CHEIN, I. "The Awareness of Self and the Structure of the Ego." *Psychological Review*, 1944, *51*, 304–314.

CHEIN, I. "The Genetic Factor in Ahistorical Psychology." *Journal of General Psychology*, 1947, *36*, 151–172.

CHILD, I. "Personality." In Vol. 5 of C. P. Stone and L. McNemar (Eds.), *Annual Review of Psychology*. Palo Alto, Calif.: Annual Reviews, 1954.

CHRISTIE, R. "Changes in Authoritarianism as Related to Situational Factors." *American Psychologist*, 1952, *7*, 307–308. (Abstract)

COCH, L., and FRENCH, J. R. P. "Overcoming Resistance to Change." *Human Relations*, 1948, *1*, 512–532.

COHN, N. *Pursuit of the Millennium*. New York: Harper and Row, 1961.

COMBS, A., and SNYGG, D. *Individual Behavior: A New Frame of Reference for Psychology*. (Rev. ed.) New York: Harper and Row, 1959.

COWEN, E. J., LANDES, J., and SCHAET, D. E. "The Effects of Mild Frustration on the Expression of Prejudiced Attitudes." *Journal of Abnormal and Social Psychology*, 1959, *58*, 33–39.

COX, C. M. *Genetic Studies of Genius*. Stanford, Calif.: Stanford University Press, 1926.

CRONBACH, L. "The Two Disciplines of Scientific Psychology" (1957). In M. Mednick and S. A. Mednick (Eds.), *Research in Personality*. New York: Holt, Rinehart, and Winston, 1963.

DEMBO, T. "Der Aeger als dynamisches problem." *Psychologische Forschung*, 1931, *15*, 1–144.

DOLLARD, J., and MILLER, N. E. *Personality and Psychotherapy*. New York: McGraw-Hill, 1950.

DUNBAR, F. *Emotions and Bodily Changes*. New York: Columbia University Press, 1938.

EAGER, J., and SMITH, M. B. "A Note on the Validity of Sanford's Authoritarian-Equalitarian Scale." *Journal of Abnormal and Social Psychology*, 1952, *47*, 265–267.

ELLIS, A. "An Operational Reformulation of Some of the Basic Principles of Psychoanalysis." In Vol. 1 of H. Feigl and M. Scriven (Eds.), *Minnesota Studies in the Philosophy of Science.* Minneapolis: University of Minnesota Press, 1956.

EMMERICH, W. "Personality Development and Concepts of Structure." *Child Development,* 1968, *39,* 671–690.

ERIKSON, E. H. *Childhood and Society.* New York: Norton, 1950.

ERIKSON, E. H. "Growth and Crises of the 'Healthy Personality'." In C. Kluckhohn, H. A. Murray, and D. M. Schneider (Eds.), *Personality in Nature, Society and Culture.* (2nd ed.) New York: Knopf, 1955.

ERIKSON, E. H. "Identity and the Life Cycle: Selected Papers." In Vol. 1 of *Psychological Issues.* New York: International Universities Press, 1959.

EYSENCK, H. *Dimensions of Personality.* London: Routledge, 1947.

EYSENCK, H. *The Scientific Study of Personality.* London: Routledge, 1952.

EYSENCK, H. *The Structure of Human Personality.* London: Methuen, 1953.

EYSENCK, H. "Learning Theory and Behavior Therapy." *Journal of Mental Science,* 1959, *105,* 61–75.

EZRIEL, H. "Experimentation Within the Psychoanalytic Session." *British Journal for the Philosophy of Science,* 1956, *1,* 29–48.

FAIRBAIRN, W. R. D. *Psychoanalytic Studies of the Personality.* London: Tavistock, 1952.

FARBER, I. E. "A Framework for the Study of Personality as a Behavioral Science." In P. Worchel and D. Byrne (Eds.), *Personality Change.* New York: Wiley, 1964.

FAWL, C. L. "Disturbances Experienced by Children in Their Natural Habitats." In R. Barker (Ed.), *The Stream of Behavior.* New York: Appleton-Century-Crofts, 1963.

FEIGL, H. "Operationism and Scientific Method." *Psychological Review,* 1945, *52,* 250–259.

FEIGL, H., and BRODBECK, M. *Readings in the Philosophy of Science.* New York: Appleton-Century-Crofts, 1953.

FEIGL, H., and SCRIVEN, M. (Eds.) *Minnesota Studies in the Philosophy of Science,* Vol. 1. Minneapolis: University of Minnesota Press, 1956.

FEIGL, H., and SELLERS, W. (Eds.) *Readings in Philosophical Analysis.* New York: Appleton-Century-Crofts, 1949.

Bibliography

FELDMAN, K. A., and NEWCOMB, T. M. *The Impact of College on Students*. San Francisco: Jossey-Bass, 1969.

FENICHEL, O. *The Psychoanalytic Theory of Neurosis*. New York: Norton, 1945.

FISHER, J. "The Memory Process and Certain Psychosocial Attitudes with Special Reference to the Law of Pragnanz." *Journal of Personality*, 1951, *19*, 406–420.

FISHER, J., and HARRIS, R. E. (Eds.) *Reinforcement Theory in Psychological Treatment—A Symposium*. Sacramento, Calif.: Bureau of Research, Department of Mental Hygiene, State of California, 1966.

FISHMAN, J. A. "Non-Intellective Factors as Predictors, as Criteria, and as Contingencies in Selection and Guidance." In T. R. McConnell (Ed.), *Selection and Educational Differentiation*. Berkeley, Calif.: Field Service Center and Center for the Study of Higher Education, University of California, 1960.

FREEDMAN, M. B. "The Passage Through College." In N. Sanford (Ed.), "Personality Development During the College Years." *Journal of Social Issues*, 1956, *12* (4).

FRENKL-BRUNSWIK, E. "Intolerance of Ambiguity as an Emotional and Perceptual Personality Variable." *Journal of Personality*, 1949, *18*, 108–143.

FRENKEL-BRUNSWIK, E. "Personality Theory and Perception." In R. R. Blake and G. V. Ramsey (Eds.), *Perception: An Approach to Personality*. New York: Ronald, 1951.

FREUD, A. *The Ego and the Mechanisms of Defense*. London: Hogarth, 1937.

FREUD, S. *The Ego and the Id*. London: Hogarth, 1927.

FREUD, S. *Civilization and Its Discontents*. London: Hogarth, 1930.

FREUD, S. *Inhibitions, Symptoms and Anxiety*. London: Hogarth, 1936.

FREUD, S. "The Interpretation of Dreams." In *The Basic Writings of Sigmund Freud*. New York: Random House, 1938. (First German edition, 1900.)

FREUD, S. *A General Introduction to Psychoanalysis* (1917). Garden City, N.Y.: Doubleday, 1943.

FREUD, S. *Collected Papers*, Vol. 2. New York: Basic Books, 1959.

FROMM, E. "Character and the Social Process." Appendix to *Escape from Freedom*. New York: Holt, Rinehart, and Winston, 1941.

FROMM, E. *Man for Himself.* New York: Holt, Rinehart, and Winston, 1947.

GIBSON, J. J. "Perception as a Function of Stimulation." In Vol. 1 of S. Koch (Ed.), *Psychology: A Study of a Science.* New York: McGraw-Hill, 1959.

GILL, M. "The Present State of Psychoanalytic Theory." *Journal of Abnormal and Social Psychology,* 1959, *58,* 1–9.

GILL, M. M., and BRENMAN, M. *Hypnosis and Related States.* New York: International Universities Press, 1959.

GOLDSTEIN, K. *The Organism.* New York: American Book, 1939.

GOLDSTEIN, K. "Functional Disturbances in Brain Damage." In S. Ariete (Ed.), *American Handbook of Psychiatry.* New York: Basic Books, 1959.

GOUGH, H. G. *California Psychological Inventory Manual.* Palo Alto, Calif.: Consulting Psychologists Press, 1957.

GRANIT, R. *Receptors and Sensory Perception.* New Haven, Conn.: Yale University Press, 1955.

GREENSON, R. R. "The Classic Psychoanalytic Approach." In S. Ariete (Ed.), *American Handbook of Psychiatry.* New York: Basic Books, 1959.

GRINKER, R. (Ed.) *Toward a Unified Theory of Human Behavior.* New York: Basic Books, 1956.

GUILFORD, J. P. *Personality.* New York: McGraw-Hill, 1959.

GUTHRIE, E. R. *The Psychology of Learning.* (Rev. ed.) New York: Harper and Row, 1952.

HALL, C., and LINDZEY, G. *Theories of Personality.* New York: Wiley, 1957.

HALL, C., and VAN DE CASTLE, R. L. "An Empirical Investigation of the Castration Complex in Dreams." *Journal of Personality,* 1965, *33,* 20–29.

HARTMANN, H. *Ego Psychology and the Problem of Adaptation* (1939). New York: International Universities Press, 1958.

HARTMANN, H., KRIS, E., and LOEWENSTEIN, R. "Comments on the Formation of Psychic Structure." In Vol. 2 of T. French and others (Eds.), *The Psychoanalytic Study of the Child.* New York: International Universities Press, 1947.

HARTSHORNE, H., and MAY, M. *Studies in Deceit.* New York: Macmillan, 1928.

HARTSHORNE, H., and MAY, M. *Studies in the Organization of Character.* New York: Macmillan, 1930.

HATHAWAY, S. R., and MCKINLEY, I. C. *The Minnesota Multiphasic Personality Inventory.* (Rev. ed.) New York: Psychological Corp., 1943.

HEBB, D. O. *The Organization of Behavior.* New York: Wiley, 1949.

HEBB, D. O. "Alice in Wonderland or Psychology Among the Biological Sciences." In H. F. Harlow and C. N. Woolsey (Eds.), *Biological and Biochemical Bases of Behavior.* Madison, Wis.: University of Wisconsin Press, 1958.

HEIDER, F. *The Psychology of Interpersonal Relations.* New York: Wiley, 1958.

HELMREICH, R., and COLLINS, B. E. "Studies in Forced Compliance: Commitment and Magnitude of Inducement to Comply as Determinants of Opinion Change." *Journal of Personality and Social Psychology,* 1968, *9,* 260–265.

HEMPEL, C. G. "A Logical Appraisal of Operationalism." *Scientific Monthly,* 1954, *79,* 215–223.

HENDRICK, I. "Instinct and the Ego During Infancy." *Psychoanalytic Quarterly,* 1942, *11,* 33–58.

HENLE, M. "An Experimental Investigation of Dynamic and Structural Determinants of Substitution." *Contributions to Psychological Theory,* 1942, *2* (7).

HENLE, M. "The Influence of Valence upon Substitution." *Journal of Psychology,* 1944, *17,* 11–19.

HILGARD, E. R. "Human Motives and the Concept of the Self." *American Psychologist,* 1949, *4,* 374–382.

HILGARD, E. R. *Introduction to Psychology.* New York: Harcourt, Brace, and World, 1953.

HILGARD, E. R. "Motivation in Learning Theory." In Vol. 5 of S. Koch (Ed.), *Psychology: A Study of a Science.* New York: McGraw-Hill, 1963.

HOLLANDER, E. P. "Authoritarianism and Leadership Choice in a Military Setting." *American Psychologist,* 1953, *8,* 368–369.

HOLT, R. R. "A Critical Examination of Freud's Concept of Bound Versus Free Cathexis." *Journal of the American Psychoanalytic Association,* 1962, *10,* 475–525.

HOLT, R. R., LUBORSKY, L., and others. *Personality Patterns of Psychiatrists,* Vols. 1 and 2. Topeka, Kan.: Menninger Foundation, 1958.

HORNEY, K. *The Neurotic Personality of Our Time.* New York: Norton, 1939.

HULL, C. L. *Principles of Behavior.* New York: Appleton-Century-Crofts, 1943.

JAHODA, M. "Toward a Social Psychology of Mental Health." In M. J. E. Senn (Ed.), *Symposium on the Healthy Personality.* New York: Josiah Macy, Jr., Foundation, 1950.

JAHODA, M. *Current Concepts of Positive Mental Health.* New York: Basic Books, 1958.

JAMES, W. *The Principles of Psychology,* Vol. 1. New York: Holt, Rinehart, and Winston, 1890.

JONES, H. E. "The California Adolescent Growth Study." *Journal of Educational Research,* 1938, *31,* 561–567.

JONES, H. E., and BAYLEY, N. "The Berkeley Growth Study." *Child Development,* 1941, *12,* 167–173.

JONES, M. R. (Ed.) *Current Theory and Research in Motivation,* Vol. 5. Lincoln, Neb.: University of Nebraska Press, 1957.

JUNG, C. G. *Contributions to Analytical Psychology.* New York: Harcourt, Brace, and World, 1928.

JUNG, C. G. *Collected Works.* Vol. 9. *Archetypes and the Collective Unconscious.* New York: Pantheon, 1954.

KAGAN, J., and MOSS, H. A. *Birth to Maturity.* New York: Wiley, 1962.

KATZ, D., and STOTLAND, E. "A Preliminary Statement to a Theory of Attitude Structure and Change." In Vol. 3 of S. Koch (Ed.), *Psychology: A Study of a Science.* New York: McGraw-Hill, 1959.

KATZ, J., and others. *No Time for Youth.* San Francisco: Jossey-Bass, 1968.

KELLY, E. L., and FISKE, D. W. *The Prediction of Performance in Clinical Psychology.* Ann Arbor, Mich.: University of Michigan Press, 1951.

KELLY, G. *The Psychology of Personal Constructs,* Vol. 1. New York: Norton, 1953.

KELMAN, H. C., and COHLER, J. "Reactions to Persuasive Communication as a Function of Cognitive Needs and Styles," *American Psychologist,* 1959, *14,* 571. (Abstract)

KENNY, D. T., and GINSBERG, R. "The Specificity of Intolerance of Ambiguity Measures." *Journal of Abnormal and Social Psychology,* 1958, *56,* 300–305.

KLEIN, G. S. "The Personal World Through Perception." In R. R. Blake and G. V. Ramsey (Eds.), *Perception: An Approach to Personality.* New York: Ronald, 1951.

KLEIN, G. S. "Perception, Motives and Personality." In J. L. McCary (Ed.), *Psychology of Personality*. Plainfield, N.J.: Logos, 1956.

KLEIN, G. S. "Tolerance for Unrealistic Experience: A Study of the Generality of Cognitive Control." *British Journal of Psychology*, 1962, *53*, 41–55.

KLEIN, G. S., and KRECH, D. "The Problem of Personality and Its Theory." *Journal of Personality*, 1951, *20*, 2–23.

KLEIN, G. S., and SCHLESINGER, H. J. "Where Is the Perceiver in Perceptual Theory?" *Journal of Personality*, 1949, *18*, 32–47.

KLEIN, M. *Contributions to Psychoanalysis, 1921–1948*. London: Hogarth, 1948.

KLOPFER, B., and KELLEY, D. M. *The Rorschach Technique*. New York: Harcourt, Brace, and World, 1946.

KLUCKHOHN, C., and MURRAY, H. A. "Personality Formation: The Determinants." In C. Kluckhohn and H. A. Murray (Eds.), *Personality in Nature, Society, and Culture*. New York: Knopf, 1948.

KOCH, S. "Behavior as 'Intrinsically' Regulated: Work Notes Toward a Pre-Theory of Phenomena Called 'Motivational'." In Vol. 4 of M. R. Jones (Ed.), *Current Theory and Research in Motivation*. Lincoln, Neb.: University of Nebraska Press, 1956.

KOCH, S. "Epilogue." In Vol. 3 of S. Koch (Ed.), *Psychology: A Study of a Science*. New York: McGraw-Hill, 1959.

KOCH, S. (Ed.) *Psychology: A Study of a Science*. New York: McGraw-Hill, 1963.

KOFKA, K. *Principles of Gestalt Psychology*. New York: Harcourt, Brace, and World, 1935.

KOHLER, W. *Gestalt Psychology*. New York: Liveright, 1929.

KOUNIN, J. "Experimental Studies of Rigidity." *Character and Personality*, 1941, *9*, 251–282.

KRECH, D., and CRUTCHFIELD, R. *Theory and Problems of Social Psychology*. New York: McGraw-Hill, 1948.

KUBIE, L. "The Fundamental Nature of the Distinction Between Normality and Neurosis." *Psychoanalytic Quarterly*, 1954, *23*, 167–204.

LANDIS, C., and BOLLES, M. *Personality and Sexuality in the Physically Handicapped Woman*. New York: Hoeber, 1942.

LAZARSFELD, P. F. "Latent Structure Analysis." In Vol. 3 of S. Koch (Ed.), *Psychology: A Study of a Science*. New York: McGraw-Hill, 1959.

LECKY, P. *Self-Consistency*. New York: Island Press Co-operative, 1945.

LEHMAN, H. C. "The Creative Years in Science and Literature." *Scientific Monthly*, 1936, *43*, 151–162.

LEVINSON, D. J. "Role, Personality and Social Structure in the Organizational Setting." *Journal of Abnormal and Social Psychology*, 1959, *58*, 170–181.

LEWIN, K. *Dynamic Theory of Personality*. New York: McGraw-Hill, 1935.

LEWIN, K. *Principles of Topological Psychology*. New York: McGraw-Hill, 1936.

LEWIN, K., DEMBO, T., FESTINGER, L., and SEARS, R. R. "Level of Aspiration." In Vol. 1 of J. M. Hunt (Ed.), *Personality and the Behavior Disorders*. New York: Ronald, 1944.

LEWIN, K., LIPPITT, R., and WHITE, R. "Patterns of Aggressive Behavior in Experimentally Created Social Climates." *Journal of Social Psychology*, 1939, *10*, 271–299.

LINDZEY, G. *Assessment of Human Motives*. New York: Holt, Rinehart, and Winston, 1958.

LINDZEY, G., and HALL, C. S. *Theories of Personality: Primary Sources and Research*. New York: Wiley, 1965.

LINTON, R. *The Cultural Background of Personality*. New York: Appleton-Century-Crofts, 1945.

LOEVINGER, J. "Measurement in Clinical Research." In B. B. Wolman (Ed.), *Handbook of Clinical Psychology*. New York: McGraw-Hill, 1965.

LOEVINGER, J. "The Meaning and Measurement of Ego Development." *American Psychologist*, 1966, *21*, 195–206.

LOEVINGER, J., and WESSLER, R. *Measuring Ego Development*, Vols. 1 and 2. San Francisco: Jossey-Bass, 1970.

LUCHINS, A. "An Evaluation of Some Current Criticisms of Gestalt Psychological Work on Perception." *Psychological Review*, 1951, *58*, 69–95.

MCCARY, J. L. (Ed.) *Psychology of Personality*. Plainfield, N.J.: Logos, 1956.

MCCLELLAND, D. C. *Personality*. New York: Holt, Rinehart, and Winston, 1951.

MCCLELLAND, D. C. "Notes for a Revised Theory of Motivation." In D. C. McClelland (Ed.), *Studies in Motivation*. New York: Appleton-Century-Crofts, 1955.

MCCLELLAND, D. C., ATKINSON, J. W., CLARKE, R. A., and LOWELL, E. J. *The Achievement Motive.* New York: Appleton-Century-Crofts, 1953.

MACCOBY, E. (Ed.) *The Development of Sex Differences.* Stanford, Calif.: Stanford University Press, 1966.

MCDOUGALL, W. *Introduction to Social Psychology.* London: Methuen, 1908.

MCDOUGALL, W. *An Outline of Psychology.* New York: Scribner's, 1923.

MCDOUGALL, W. *The Energies of Men.* London: Methuen, 1932.

MACFARLANE, J. W. "The Life-Career Approach to the Study of Personality Development: Some Findings from a Thirty-Year Longitudinal Study." Berkeley, Calif.: Institute of Human Development, 1960.

MACFARLANE, J. W., ALLEN, L., and HONZIK, M. P. "A Developmental Study of the Behavior Problems of Normal Children Between Twenty-One Months and Fourteen Years." *University of California Publications in Child Development,* 1954.

MACKINNON, D. W. "The Structure of Personality." In J. M. Hunt (Ed.), *Personality and the Behavior Disorders.* New York: Ronald, 1944.

MACKINNON, D. W. "Applications of Clinical Psychology to Assessment." In D. Brower and L. E. Abt (Eds.), *Progress in Clinical Psychology.* New York: Grune and Stratton, 1952.

MACKINNON, D. W. "Fact and Fancy in Personality Research." *American Psychologist,* 1953, *8,* 138–146.

MACKINNON, D. W., and MASLOW, A. H. "Personality." In H. Helson (Ed.), *Theoretical Foundations of Psychology.* Princeton, N.J.: Van Nostrand, 1951.

MADISON, P. *Freud's Concept of Repression and Defense, Its Theoretical and Observational Language.* Minneapolis: University of Minnesota Press, 1961.

MADISON, P. *Personality Development in College.* Reading, Mass.: Addison-Wesley, 1969.

MANN, L., and JANIS, I. L. "A Follow-Up Study on the Long Term Effects of Emotional Role Playing." *Journal of Personality and Social Psychology,* 1968, *8,* 339–342.

MARCUSE, H. *One Dimensional Man.* Boston: Beacon Press, 1964.

MASLOW, A. H. "Problem-Centering vs. Means-Centering in Science." *Philosophy of Science,* 1946, *13,* 326–331.

MASLOW, A. H. "Self-Actualizing People: A Study of Psychological Health." *Personality: Symposia on Topical Issues,* 1950 (I).

MASLOW, A. H. *Motivation and Personality.* New York: Harper and Row, 1954.

MASLOW, A. H. "Deficiency Motivation and Growth Motivation." In Vol. 3 of M. R. Jones (Ed.), *Current Theory and Research in Motivation.* Lincoln, Neb.: University of Nebraska Press, 1955.

MATTARAZZO, J. D. "Psychotherapeutic Processes." In *Annual Review of Psychology.* Palo Alto, Calif.: Annual Reviews, 1965.

MAY, R. "The Existential Approach." In S. Ariete (Ed.), *American Handbook of Psychiatry.* New York: Basic Books, 1959.

MAY, R., ANGEL, E., and ELLENBERGER, H. F. *Existence: A New Dimension in Psychiatry and Psychology.* New York: Basic Books, 1958.

MAZE, J. R. "On Some Corruptions of the Doctrine of Homeostasis." *Psychological Review,* 1953, *60,* 405–412.

MEEHL, P. "Wanted: A Good Cook-Book." *American Psychologist,* 1956, *11,* 263–272.

MEEHL, P. W., and MACCORQUODALE, K. "On a Distinction Between Hypothetical Constructs and Intervening Variables." *Psychological Review,* 1948, *55,* 95–107.

MILLER, J. G. "Unconscious Processes and Perception." In R. R. Blake and G. V. Ramsey (Eds.), *Perception: An Approach to Personality.* New York: Ronald, 1951.

MILLER, J. G. "Toward a General Theory for the Behavioral Sciences." *American Psychologist,* 1955, *10,* 513–531.

MILLER, J. G. "Information Input Overload and Psychopathology." *American Journal of Psychiatry,* 1960, *116,* 695–704.

MILLER, N. E. "Liberalization of Basic S-R Concepts: Extensions to Conflict Behavior, Motivation and Social Learning." In Vol. 2 of S. Koch (Ed.), *Psychology: A Study of a Science.* New York: McGraw-Hill, 1959.

MITTELMAN, B., WOLFF, H. G., and SCHORF, M. "Emotions and Gastroduodenal Functions." *Psychosomatic Medicine,* 1942, *4,* 5–61.

MOWRER, O. H. *Learning Theory and Personality Dynamics.* New York: Ronald, 1950.

MOWRER, O. H. *Psychotherapy: Theory and Research.* New York: Ronald, 1953.

MOWRER, O. H. *Learning Theory and Behavior.* New York: Wiley, 1960.

MURPHY, G. *Personality: A Biosocial Approach to Origins and Structure.* New York: Harper and Row, 1947.

MURPHY, G. "Introduction." In H. A. Witkin and others, *Personality Through Perception.* New York: Harper and Row, 1953.

MURPHY, G. *Human Potentialities.* New York: Basic Books, 1958.

MURPHY, G., and JENSEN, F. *Approaches to Personality.* New York: Harper and Row, 1932.

MURRAY, H. A. "The Effects of Fear upon Estimates of the Maliciousness of Other Personalities." *Journal of Social Psychology,* 1933, *4,* 310–329.

MURRAY, H. A. *Explorations in Personality.* New York: Oxford, 1938.

MURRAY, H. A. "Introduction to Melville's *Pierre.*" In H. Melville, *Pierre.* New York: Farrar, Straus, and Giroux, 1949.

MURRAY, H. A. "Toward a Classification of Interaction." In T. Parsons and E. A. Shils (Eds.), *Toward a General Theory of Action.* Cambridge, Mass.: Harvard University Press, 1951.

MURRAY, H. A. "Preparations for the Scaffold of a Comprehensive System." In Vol. 3 of S. Koch (Ed.), *Psychology: A Study of a Science.* New York: McGraw-Hill, 1959.

MURRAY, H. A., and KLUCKHOHN, C. "Outline of a Conception of Personality." In C. Kluckhohn and H. A. Murray (Eds.), *Personality in Nature, Society, and Culture.* New York: Knopf, 1948.

MURRAY, H. A., and KLUCKHOHN, C. "Outline of a Conception of Personality." In C. Kluckhohn, H. A. Murray, and D. M. Schneider (Eds.), *Personality in Nature, Society, and Culture.* (2nd ed.) New York: Knopf, 1955.

NEWCOMB, T. M. "Role Behavior in the Study of Individual Personality and of Groups." *Journal of Personality,* 1950, *18,* 273–290. (a)

NEWCOMB, T. M. *Social Psychology.* New York: Holt, Rinehart, and Winston, 1950. (b)

NEWCOMB, T. M. "Attitude Development as a Function of Reference Groups: The Bennington Study." In E. Maccoby, T. M. Newcomb, and E. J. Hartley (Eds.), *Readings in Social Psychology.* New York: Holt, Rinehart, and Winston, 1958.

OLDS, J. "A Physiological Study of Reward." In D. McClelland (Ed.), *Studies in Motivation.* New York: Appleton-Century-Crofts, 1955.

OLDS, J., and MILNER, P. "Positive Reinforcement Produced by Electrical Stimulation of Septal Area and Other Regions of Rat Brain." *Journal of Comparative and Physiological Psychology,* 1954, *47,* 419–427.

OSGOOD, C. E. "Behavior Theory and the Social Sciences." *Behavioral Science,* 1956, *1,* 167–185.

OSGOOD, C. E. "Motivational Dynamics of Language Behavior." In Vol. 5 of M. R. Jones (Ed.), *Current Theory and Research in Motivation.* Lincoln, Neb.: University of Nebraska Press, 1957.

OSS Assessment Staff. *Assessment of Men.* New York: Holt, Rinehart, and Winston, 1948.

OVSIANKINA, M. "Die Wiederaufnahme von unterbrochener Handlungen." *Psychologische Forschung,* 1928, *11,* 302–382.

PACE, C. R., and STERN, G. "An Approach to the Measurement of the Psychological Characteristics of College Environments." *Journal of Educational Psychology,* 1958, *49,* 269–277.

PARSONS, T., BALES, R. F., and SHILS, E. A. *Working Papers in the Theory of Action.* New York: Free Press, 1953.

PARSONS, T., and SHILS, E. A. (Eds.) *Toward a General Theory of Action.* Cambridge, Mass.: Harvard University Press, 1952.

PENFIELD, W. "The Permanent Record of the Stream of Consciousness." *Proceedings of the Fourteenth International Congress of Psychology,* 1955.

PENFIELD, W., and JASPER, A. *Epilepsy and the Functional Anatomy of the Human Brain.* Boston: Little, Brown, 1954.

PHILLIPSON, H. *The Object Relations Technique (with tests).* New York: Free Press, 1956.

PLAUT, T. F. A. (Ed.) *Alcohol Problems: A Report to the Nation.* New York: Oxford University Press, 1967.

POSTMAN, L. Review of H. A. Witken and others, *Personality Through Perception. Psychological Bulletin,* 1955, *52,* 79–83.

POSTMAN, L., BRUNER, J. S., and MCGINNIES, E. "Personal Values as Selective Factors in Perception." *Journal of Abnormal and Social Psychology,* 1948, *43,* 142–154.

Proceedings of the Fourteenth International Congress of Psychology, 1954.

PROSHANSKY, H., and MURPHY, G. "The Effects of Reward and Punishment on Perception." *Journal of Psychology*, 1942, *13*, 295–305.

PROTHRO, E. T., and MELIKIAN, L. "The California Public Opinion Scale in an Authoritarian Culture." *Public Opinion Quarterly*, 1953, *17*, 353–362.

PUMPIAN-MINDLIN, E. "Propositions Concerning Energic-Economic Aspects of Libido Theory." In L. Bellak (Ed.), "Conceptual and Methodological Problems in Psychoanalysis." *Annals of the New York Academy of Sciences*, 1959, *76*, Art. 4.

RAIMY, V. C. "Self-Reference in Counseling Interviews." *Journal of Consulting Psychology*, 1948, *12*, 153–163.

RAPAPORT, D. *Emotions and Memory*. Baltimore: Williams and Wilkins, 1942.

RAPAPORT, D. "The Theory of Ego Autonomy: A Generalization." *Bulletin of the Menninger Clinic*, 1958, *22*, 13–35.

RAPAPORT, D. "The Structure of Psychoanalytic Theory: A Systematizing Attempt." In Vol. 3 of S. Koch (Ed.), *Psychology: A Study of a Science*. New York: McGraw-Hill, 1959.

RITTER, W. E. *The Unity of the Organism*. Boston: Badger, 1919.

ROGERS, C. R. *Client-Centered Therapy: Its Current Practice, Implications, and Theory*. Boston: Houghton Mifflin, 1951.

ROGERS, C. R. "A Theory of Therapy, Personality, and Interpersonal Relationships, as Developed in the Client-Centered Framework." In Vol. 3 of S. Koch (Ed.), *Psychology: A Study of a Science*. New York: McGraw-Hill, 1959.

ROGERS, C. R., and DYMOND, R. (Eds.) *Psychotherapy and Personality Change*. Chicago: University of Chicago Press, 1954.

ROKEACH, M. "Generalized Mental Rigidity as a Factor in Ethnocentrism." *Journal of Abnormal and Social Psychology*, 1948, *43*, 259–278.

ROKEACH, M. *The Open and Closed Mind*. New York: Basic Books, 1960.

ROSENZWEIG, S. "The Ghost of Henry James: A Study in Thematic Apperception." In C. Kluckhohn, H. A. Murray, and D. M. Schneider (Eds.), *Personality in Nature, Society, and Culture*. (2nd ed.) New York: Knopf, 1955.

RUBINSTEIN, E. A., and PARLOFF, M. B. (Eds.) *Research in Psychotherapy*. Washington, D. C.: American Psychological Association, 1959.

RUDIKOFF, E. C. "A Comparative Study of the Changes in the Concepts of the Self, the Ordinary Person, and the Ideal in Eight Cases." In C. R. Rogers and R. F. Dymond (Eds.), *Psychotherapy and Personality Change*. Chicago: University of Chicago Press, 1954.

RUSSEL, E. S. *Form and Function*. London: Murray, 1916.

SAHAKIAN, W. S. *Psychology of Personality: Readings in Theory*. Chicago: Rand McNally, 1965.

SANFORD, N. "The Effects of Abstinence from Food upon Imaginal Processes: A Preliminary Experiment." *Journal of Psychology*, 1937, *3*, 145–159.

SANFORD, N. "Individual and Social Change in a Community under Pressure: The Oath Controversy." *Journal of Social Issues*, 1953, *9*, 25–42.

SANFORD, N. "The Dynamics of Identification." *Psychological Review*, 1955, *62*, 106–118.

SANFORD, N. "The Approach of *The Authoritarian Personality*." In J. L. McCary (Ed.), *The Psychology of Personality*. Plainfield, N.J.: Logos, 1956. (a)

SANFORD, N. (Ed.) "Personality Development During the College Years." *Journal of Social Issues*, 1956, *4*, 3–70. (b)

SANFORD, N. "Surface and Depth in the Individual Personality." *Psychological Review*, 1956, *63*, 349–359. (c)

SANFORD, N. "Our Students Today: Individualists or Conformers." Berkeley, Calif.: Institute of Personality Assessment and Research, University of California, 1957.

SANFORD, N. "The Impact of a Woman's College on Its Students." In A. E. Traxler (Ed.), *Long-Range Planning for Education*. Washington, D. C.: American Council on Education, 1958. (a)

SANFORD, N. "Social Science and Social Reform." *Journal of Social Issues*, 1958, *21*, 54–70. (b)

SANFORD, N. "Developmental Status of the Entering Freshman." In N. Sanford (Ed.), *The American College*. New York: Wiley, 1962. (Paperback, 1967.)

SANFORD, N. *Self and Society*. New York: Atherton, 1966.

SANFORD, N. "Decline of Individualism." *Public Health Reports*, 1970, in press.

SANFORD, N., and others. "Physique, Personality and Scholarship." *Monographs of Social Research in Child Development*, 1943, *8* (1).

SANFORD, N., and others. "The Findings of the Commission in Psychology." *Annals of the New York Academy of Sciences,* 1955, *63,* 341–364.

SAPIR, E. "Personality." In *Encyclopedia of the Social Sciences,* Vol. 12. New York: Macmillan, 1934.

SARBIN, T. R. "A Preface to a Psychological Analysis of the Self." *Psychological Review,* 1952, *59,* 11–22.

SARNOFF, I. *Personality Dynamics and Development.* New York: Wiley, 1962.

SARNOFF, I., and KATZ, D. "The Motivational Basis of Attitude Change." *Journal of Abnormal and Social Psychology,* 1954, *49,* 115–124.

SCHJELDERUP, H. "Lasting Effects of Psychoanalytic Treatment." *Psychiatry,* 1955, *18,* 109–133.

SCOTT, W. A. "Research Definitions of Mental Health and Mental Illness." *Psychological Bulletin,* 1958, *55,* 67–87.

SCRIVEN, M. "A Study of Radical Behaviorism." In Vol. 1 of H. Feigl and M. Scriven (Eds.), *Minnesota Studies in the Philosophy of Science.* Minneapolis: University of Minnesota Press, 1956.

SEARS, R. R. "Personality." In C. P. Stone (Ed.), *Annual Review of Psychology.* Palo Alto, Calif.: Annual Reviews, 1950.

SEARS, R. R. "Social Behavior and Personality Development." In T. Parsons and E. A. Shils (Eds.), *Toward a General Theory of Action.* Cambridge, Mass.: Harvard University Press, 1951. (a)

SEARS, R. R. "A Theoretical Framework for Personality and Social Behavior." *American Psychologist,* 1951, *6,* 476–482. (b)

SEEMAN, J., and RASKIN, N. J. "Research Perspectives in Client-Centered Therapy." In O. H. Mowrer (Ed.), *Psychotherapy: Theory and Research.* New York: Ronald, 1953.

SELYE, H. "The General Adaptation Syndrome and the Diseases of Adaptation." *Journal of Clinical Endocrinology and Metabolism,* 1946, *2,* 117–230.

SENN, M. J. E. (Ed.) *Symposium on the Healthy Personality.* New York: Josiah Macy, Jr., Foundation, 1950.

SHAFFER, L. F., and SHOHEN, E. J. *Psychology of Adjustment.* (2nd ed.) Boston: Houghton Mifflin, 1956.

SHAKOW, D., and RAPAPORT, D. "The Influence of Freud on American Psychology." *Psychological Issues,* 1964, *4* (3).

SHEERER, M. "Cognitive Theory." In G. Lindzey (Ed.), *Handbook of Social Psychology*. Reading, Mass.: Addison-Wesley, 1954.

SHELDON, W. *The Varieties of Human Physique: An Introduction to Constitutional Psychology*. New York: Harper and Row, 1940.

SHELDON, W. (with C. W. Dupertius and E. McDermott). *Atlas of Men: A Guide for Somatotyping the Adult Male at All Ages*. New York: Harper and Row, 1954.

SHERIF, M. *The Psychology of Social Norms*. New York: Harper and Row, 1936.

SHERIF, M., and CANTRIL, H. *The Psychology of Ego-Involvements*. New York: Wiley, 1947.

SHOCK, N. "Physiological Factors in Behavior." In Vol. 1 of J. M. Hunt (Ed.), *Personality and the Behavior Disorders*. New York: Ronald, 1944.

SKINNER, B. F. "Are Theories of Learning Necessary?" *Psychological Review*, 1950, *57*, 193–216.

SMITH, M. B. "The Phenomenological Approach in Personality Theory: Some Critical Remarks." *Journal of Abnormal and Social Psychology*, 1950, *45*, 516–522.

SMITH, M. B. "Research Strategies Toward a Conception of Positive Mental Health." *American Psychologist*, 1959, *14*, 673–681.

SMITH, M. B., BRUNER, J., and WHITE, R. W. *Opinions and Personality*. New York, Wiley, 1956.

SMUTS, F. C. *Holism and Evolution*. New York: Macmillan, 1926.

SPENCE, K. W. "The Nature of Theory Construction in Contemporary Psychology." *Psychological Review*, 1944, *57*, 47–68.

STAGNER, R. *Psychology of Personality*. New York: McGraw-Hill, 1948.

STAGNER, R. "Homeostasis as a Unifying Concept in Personality Theory." *Psychological Review*, 1951, *58*, 5–17.

STAGNER, R. "Homeostasis: Corruptions or Misconceptions?—A Reply." *Psychological Review*, 1954, *61*, 205–208.

STAGNER, R. "Theories of Personality." In B. B. Wolman (Ed.), *Handbook of Clinical Psychology*. New York: McGraw-Hill, 1965.

STEIN, M. "Explorations in Typology." In R. W. White (Ed.), *The Study of Lives*. New York: Atherton, 1963.

STEINER, I. D. "Reactions to Adverse and Favorable Evaluations of One's Self." *Journal of Personality*, 1968, *36*, 553–562.

STEPHENSON, W. *The Study of Behavior*. Chicago: University of Chicago Press, 1953.

STERN, G. S., STEIN, M., and BLOOM, B. S. *Methods in Personality Assessment*. New York: Free Press, 1956.

STERN, W. *General Psychology from the Personalistic Standpoint*. New York: Macmillan, 1938.

SULLIVAN, H. S. *The Interpersonal Theory of Psychiatry*. New York: Norton, 1953.

SYMONDS, P. M. *The Dynamics of Human Adjustment*. New York: Appleton-Century-Crofts, 1946.

SYMONDS, P. M. *The Ego and the Self*. New York: Appleton-Century-Crofts, 1951.

SZASZ, T. S. "A Critical Analysis of Some Aspects of the Libido Theory." In L. Bellack (Ed.), "Conceptual and Methodological Problems in Psychoanalysis." *Annals of the New York Academy of Sciences*, 1959, *76*, Art. 4.

SZASZ, T. S. "The Myth of Mental Illness." *American Psychologist*, 1960, *15*, 113–118.

TAYLOR, J. A. "The Relationship of Anxiety to the Conditioned Eyelid Response." *Journal of Experimental Psychology*, 1951, *41*, 81–92.

TERMAN, L. M., and ODEN, M. H. *The Gifted Child Grows Up*. Stanford, Calif.: Stanford University Press, 1947.

TERMAN, L. M., and ODEN, M. H. *The Gifted Group at Mid-Life: Thirty-Five Years' Follow-Up of the Superior Child*. Stanford, Calif.: Stanford University Press, 1959.

THISTLETHWAIT, D. "College Environments and the Development of Talent." *Science*, 1959, *130*, 71–76.

TOLMAN, E. C. "Operational Behaviorism and Current Trends in Psychology." *Proceedings of the Twenty-Fifth Anniversary Celebration of the Inauguration of Graduate Studies*. Los Angeles: University of Southern California Press, 1936.

TOLMAN, E. C. "The Determiners of Behavior at a Choice Point." *Psychological Review*, 1938, *45*, 1–41.

TOLMAN, E. C. "Cognitive Maps in Rats and Men." *Psychological Review*, 1948, *55*, 189–208.

TOLMAN, E. C. "A Psychological Model." In T. Parsons and E. A. Shils (Eds.), *Toward a General Theory of Action*. Cambridge, Mass.: Harvard University Press, 1951.

TOLMAN, E. C. "Principles of Purposive Behavior." In Vol. 2 of S. Koch (Ed.), *Psychology: A Study of a Science.* New York: McGraw-Hill, 1959.

TOMKINS, S. S. *The Thematic Apperception Test: The Theory and Technique of Interpretation.* New York: Grune and Stratton, 1947.

TOMKINS, S. S. *Consciousness, Imagery, and Affect.* New York: Springer, 1961.

VON BERTALANFFY, L. "An Outline of General Systems Theory." *British Journal of Philosophy and Science,* 1950, *1,* 134–165.

VON BERTALANFFY, L. "Theoretical Models in Biology and Psychology." *Journal of Personality,* 1951, *20,* 24–38.

WALLACH, H. "Some Considerations Concerning the Relation Between Perception and Cognition." *Journal of Personality,* 1949, *18,* 6–13.

WEBSTER, H., and HEIST, P. "Construction of a Multiple Trait Personality Test for Use with College Populations." Berkeley, Calif.: Center for the Study of Higher Education, University of California, 1959.

WERNER, H. *Comparative Psychology of Mental Development.* (Rev. ed.) Chicago: Follett, 1948.

WHEELER, R. H. *The Science of Psychology.* (2nd ed.) New York: Crowell, 1940.

WHITE, R. W. *The Abnormal Personality.* New York: Ronald, 1948.

WHITE, R. W. *Lives in Progress.* New York: Holt, Rinehart, and Winston, 1952.

WHITE, R. W. Review of D. C. McClelland, J. W. Atkinson, R. A. Clark, and E. J. Lowell, *The Achievement Motive. Psychological Bulletin,* 1955, *52,* 95–97.

WHITE, R. W. "Motivation Reconsidered: The Concept of Competence." *Psychological Review,* 1959, *66,* 297–333.

WHITE, R. W. "Ego and Reality in Psychoanalytic Theory," *Psychological Issues,* 1963, *3* (3). (a)

WHITE, R. W. (Ed.) *The Study of Lives.* New York: Atherton, 1963. (b)

WHITEHORN, J. C. "Goals of Psychotherapy." In E. A. Rubinstein and M. B. Parloff (Eds.), *Research in Psychotherapy.* Washington, D. C.: American Psychological Association, 1959.

WHITING, J. M. W., and CHILD, I. L. *Child Training and Personality.* New Haven, Conn.: Yale University Press, 1953.

WILSON, B. "Response to Nevitt Sanford." In W. R. Niblett (Ed.), *Higher Education: Demand and Response*. London: Tavistock, 1969. San Francisco: Jossey-Bass, 1970.

WITKIN, H. A., and others. *Personality Through Perception*. New York: Harper and Row, 1953.

WOLPE, J. *Psychotherapy by Reciprocal Inhibition*. Stanford, Calif.: Stanford University Press, 1958.

WRIGHT, B. A. "Altruism in Children and the Perceived Conduct of Others." *Journal of Abnormal and Social Psychology*, 1942, *37*, 218–233.

ZAMANSKY, H. S. "An Investigation of the Psychoanalytic Theory of Paranoid Delusions." *Journal of Personality*, 1958, *26*, 410–425.

ZEIGNARNIK, B. "Über das Behalten von erledigten und unerledigten Handlungen." *Psychologische Forschung*, 1927, *9*, 1–85.

ZIGLER, E., BALLA, D., and BUTTERFIELD, E. C. "A Longitudinal Investigation of the Relationship Between Preinstitutional Social Deprivation and Social Motivation in Institutionalized Retardates." *Journal of Personality and Social Psychology*, 1968, *10*, 437–445.

Name Index

A

ADAMS, D., 2, 3, 8
ADELSON, J., 3
ADLER, A., 131, 133
ADORNO, T. W., 23, 64, 75
ALFERT, E., 85
ALLEN, L., 25, 42
ALLPORT, G. W., 7, 9, 10, 16, 17, 18, 27, 34, 37, 46, 51, 57, 69, 70, 76, 88, 94, 95, 108, 116, 117, 118, 121, 124, 141
ANGEL, E., 55
ANGYAL, A., 7, 13, 18, 75, 81, 127
ASCH, S. E., 23, 26, 87, 141
ASHBY, R. W., 49, 59

B

BALES, R. R., 21
BALINT, M., 26
BALLA, D., 89
BARKER, R. G., 82, 105, 108, 122
BARON, F., 14, 25, 26

BARTLETT, F. C., 23
BAYLEY, N., 89
BERMANN, G., 38, 39
BERTOCCI, P. A., 27
BETTELHEIM, B., 63, 105
BLOCK, J., 85
BLOOM, B. S., 25, 89, 105
BOLLES, M., 107
BOTT, E., 105
BRAND, H., 20
BRENMAN, M., 69
BRIDGEMAN, P. W., 39
BRONFENBRENNER, J., 8, 10
BROWN, D., 105
BROWNFAIN, J. J., 32
BRUNER, J. S., 6, 21, 23
BRUNSWIK, E., 122, 140
BÜHLER, C., 112, 153, 154
BÜHLER, K., 55
BULLARD, D. M., 117
BURTON, A., 117
BURWEN, L. S., 37
BUTTERFIELD, E. C., 89

Subject Index

General psychology (*Cont.*)
  personological approach to,
  125–131; relations of personality to, 120–131, 137; subject
  matter of, 140–141
General systems theory, 10, 35, 44,
  102
General theories of behavior. *See*
  General psychological theory
Gestalt psychology, 122, 127
Gestalt theories, 16, 17, 25, 35, 44,
  51

H

Habit, 16, 22; as hypothetical construct, 94–95; psychology, 37
Harvard Psychological Clinic, 25,
  112, 143
Higher mental processes, 25, 26, 27,
  44, 52, 92
Historical causation, 113–114
Holism, 6–9, 11, 31, 32, 34, 44, 76,
  77, 78, 92, 118. *See also* Organismic point of view
Holistic approach, 118
Holistic conception of personality,
  7
Holistic theorists, 134
Holistic thinkers, 127
Homeostasis, 50, 52, 53–54, 88. *See
  also* Tension-reduction theory
Hypothetical constructs, 39, 40, 41

I

Id, 11, 16, 24, 57, 68, 69, 78
Identity of organism, 21. *See also*
  Ego identity
Individual differences, 42, 113
Individual personalities, study of:
  in clinical diagnosis, 117; in
  personality assessment, 117
Inferred self, 29–30, 70
Institute of Personality Assessment
  and Research, University of
  California, 128
Integration of personality, 4
Interpersonal relations, 101
Interpersonal situations, 10
Intervening variables, 40, 96–97

K

Kleinian psychoanalysis, 58, 62

L

Learning, 123–124
Leibnizian tradition in psychology,
  57
Levels of analysis, 139–140, 142
Life span, 139; as unit for study, 7,
  81, 112
Lockean tradition in psychology, 57

M

Method centeredness, 41, 42, 130
Minnesota Multiphasic Personality
  Inventory, 14, 75
Molar behavior, 40, 139
Motivation, 120–121
Motive, 22–23, 43; drive reduction,
  27; growth, 27

N

Needs, 17, 22, 52; cognitive, 23;
  conflict of, 51; fundamental,
  23; prepotent, 52
New York University Research Center for Mental Health, 128

O

Office of Strategic Services assessment work, 14, 24
Operationism, 39–40, 96
Organism as a whole, distinguished
  from personality, 106–107
Organismic laws, 137
Organismic point of view, 6, 7, 18,
  31, 34, 44, 76, 115, 126–127,
  130–131; implications of for
  relations of general and personality psychology, 137–143;
  limitations upon, 130; methodological consequences of,
  143; methodology adequate
  to, 127; opposition to, 130.
  See also Holism
Organization of personality, 9, 10,
  11, 32

P

Person-environment system as unit
  for study, 101

Phenomenal self, 29–31
Physiological model of personality processes, 59, 101–102
Physiological variables and personality, 107–108
Physique and personality, 107–108
Process activity, 55
Professional behavior of psychologists, 143
Projective techniques, 42, 80, 81
"Psychiatric" definition of personality, 131
Psychoanalysis, 19, 24, 25, 26, 28, 51, 69, 70, 72, 73, 78, 82, 127; and behaviorism, 25, 26, 55, 57, 58, 59, 86, 87, 88, 91; and Gestalt psychology, 35; and operationism, 40; and phenomenal self, 28, 29; and theory, 16, 43, 67, 80, 86, 87; and writers, 11, 70, 76
Psychoanalytic concepts, objective studies of, 136
Psychoanalytic institutes, 115
Psychoanalytic theories, 135–136; declining interest in, 136
Psychological environment, 102–104; role of in personality theory, 103–104
Psychosomatic relationships, 108
Psychotherapy, 19, 26, 38, 82, 85, 88, 98–100; follow-up studies of, 3, 98; research on, 97
Purpose as organizer of behavior, 125–126

R

Reductionism, 126–127, 138
Regnant processes, 71
Role behavior and personality, 9

S

Salzburg Seminar in American Studies, 58
Self: and ego, 27–31, 44, 92; as system, 29
Self-concept, 16, 27, 62, 63, 121
Self of awareness, 29–30
Sex differences in perception, 142
Size of analytic category, 33, 38

Social determinants and personality, 36
Social environment and personality, 9, 60
Social psychology, 141
Social stimulus value, 100
Social structure and personality, 105–106
Social theory, 135
Social worker, 104–105
Sociology, 19, 36, 44
Somatotypes, 107–108
Specialization in personality research, 132
Stimulus-response, 59; elements, 15, 52; theory, 15, 16, 52, 87. See also Behavior theory
Structure: change in, 86–90; definition of, 46, 90; of personality, 45; stability of, 86–90
Superego, 11, 16, 68, 78; cultural elements of, 65–66
Systematic causation, 113–114

T

Teaching of psychology, 137
Teleology and psychological theory, 49
Tension-reduction theory, 21, 22, 52–56, 76, 88, 90, 135; modes of, 8. See also Homeostasis
Theories of personality, 126
Time perspective of personality, 11
Traits, 18, 19; common, 118–119; ideographic, 118; instrumental, 22; rare, 119
Trends in personality theories, 43

U

Unconscious processes, 24, 68, 71, 72–77, 87, 115
Uniqueness of personality, 8, 10, 11, 17, 116–119, 120–121; critique of Allport's doctrine of, 117–119

W

Ways of dividing personality, 14–17
Whole personality, study of, 118–119, 125